*I don't know of any other traveler who has immersed himself in the world so much or for so long. If he says these are the rules of travel, you'd be a fool not to follow them.* — Peter Moore, Author of *The Wrong Way Home*

*For 16 years, Andy has been known as "foreigner," traveling overland across continents, making friends, learning local customs, and showing the world as it is. Through it all, he's always shown the way for others to follow. Andy Graham blazed the trail that all modern perpetual travelers follow.* — Wade Shepard, Author of *Ghost Cities of China* and owner of VagabondJourney.com

*Andy Graham has been traveling and living abroad for over 16 years, and his book reflects a no-nonsense approach that succeeds in imparting practical and invaluable gems useful for anyone at any level of experience. Andy has written The Rules of Travel having, by his own admission, made nearly every mistake possible while learning from the process with the demonstrated intent to pass along his unvarnished wisdom.* — Gregory Hubbs, Editor-in-Chief of TransitionsAbroad.com

*I've known Andy as an avid indie traveler for over a decade now. Through that time, I've known him to always seek the truth, help and inspire folks to go get a life, and do some long-term travel. Buy his book and download his wisdom onto your mental hard drive.* — Sean E. Keener, CEO of BootsnAll.com and AirTreks.com

*If you walk through a minefield, it's best to follow in someone else's footsteps. Andy is the only person I'm aware of who's traveled the world for 16 years continuously. For those wanting time-tested knowledge prior to launching a journey, this is your book.* — Eric Clearwater

D0840412

## Ask Andy Show, YouTube

Andy Lee Graham produces 3-10 videos daily for his *Ask Andy Show* on YouTube channel HoboTraveler. On the show, Andy offers his expert advice, responding to audience-posted questions about travel, real estate, being happy … He'll offer up an opinion on anything and everything. And he is continuously reporting about the real people and situations he meets in exotic countries.

Follow the Hobo Traveler channel on YouTube at Youtube.com/user/HoboTraveler or visit HoboTraveler.com to read his cavalier, often cheeky observations on topics that other traveler writers are too timid to touch.

## Hobo Traveler Products, Amazon.com

In 2013, Andy started selling travel products on Amazon.com – necessary travel gear, not for sale anywhere else. These are his own inventions, innovations, and adaptations – travel gear Andy actually carries in his backpack. He refuses to recommend or sell anything that he does not use himself. Enter his Amazon.com storefront by visiting: TheRulesOfTravel.com/amazon

# The Rules of Travel
## Think Twice Before Crossing the Rules

## Volume I

# The Rules of Travel
## Think Twice Before Crossing the Rules

## Volume I

## Andy Lee Graham

Real Travelers Press
Orland, Indiana
2014

Real Travelers Press
9545 West 120 No 26
Orland, IN 46776-0026
realtravelerspress.com

ISBN-10: 0990330702
ISBN-13: 978-0-9903307-0-7

Cover design by Alan Oak (www.alanoak.com).

# Contents

# Foreword

There's no shortage of budget travel advice out there in print and online. The worst of it comes from junior editors in a New York City cubicle who rarely travel. A step up from that is advice from round-the-world backpackers who are on their first trip away from home and are figuring it all out as they go. Complicating the problem is the fact that most travel magazines, websites, and blogs depend at least in part on direct advertising from the travel industry. There's a good reason you never see a bad hotel review in Travel + Leisure: Many of their big-spending advertisers are hotel chains. The magazine is owned by American Express, who certainly doesn't want you staying in a $10 hotel owned by a single family. Travel is a huge industry – perhaps the world's largest – with lots of marketers chasing those spending money on vacations.

By nature though, budget travelers are fragmented and finicky, independent and difficult to put into a marketing box. So if you're a long-term traveler on a tight budget, you probably won't find much in the mainstream travel media world that speaks to you. You can find plenty of blogs, but many give advice that is dubious at best, downright dangerous at worst. So we must hunt for authentic voices outside the mainstream. We must find real travelers we can trust, people who measure their travels in years and their passport stamps in dozens – over a long enough period that they weren't just checking off boxes and posting status updates. We need to find writers who have traveled on $20 a day, have lived in multiple countries, and who have a very strong bullshit meter.

Andy Graham is one of those travelers, the most genuine one I know. I've met Andy before and spoken to him by phone and email at least 50 times. We may not agree 100 percent of the time on every bullet point in this book, but I know if I challenge him on something, he'll be able to explain his point of view clearly. He'll probably throw in a good story too about what happened to him one time in Togo or Thailand.

He's been to places that are so far off the tourist trail that "the beaten path" is a day's bus ride away. He has supported himself for more than a decade on the road, writing about his experiences on multiple continents. He's a slow traveler that gets to know a place well. He travels on a budget, but knows when to spend to get a great value. He is never afraid to engage with the people who live in a place, but will never let them make him a victim or a pushover.

If you want to read a travel book that will minimize your problems, keep you out of trouble, and save you a fortune no matter where you're headed, heed *The Rules of Travel*. The advice in here will make you savvy and secure, while saving you money and time.

— Tim Leffel

*Tim Leffel is a travel writer who has dispatched articles from five continents over a 20-year period. He is the author of four books, including* The World's Cheapest Destinations. *You can find his regular rants and advice on CheapestDestinationsBlog.com or see the award-winning narrative webzine he edits, PerceptiveTravel.com. He currently lives in Guanajauto, Mexico, with his family.*

# Preface

*A foolish consistency is the hobgoblin of little minds, adored by little statesmen and philosophers and divines.* — Ralph Waldo Emerson, "Self-Reliance"

This book – and most words written by me, Andy Lee Graham – were written while sleeping in a strange hotel on the other side of the planet. And, yes, I took all the photos; each one has a memory and story. This is a book written by a traveler who never stopped to write a book, because I am a traveler first and a writer second. Travel is my life, a paradise of sorts. I refuse to stop, even to write books.

After sleeping in over 1,000 hotels and writing 8,000 travel Internet blog posts, many of which were travel tips, it became time to find more clarity. And printing a book is a commitment to clear words. There is no way to erase what I have written, and I must commit to my words. Yet my first notion was to call the rules "guidelines"; however, people don't take guidelines seriously, and the word "rule" makes travelers think twice before they break them.

Real travelers learn to look twice, often 4-5 times, before crossing the road. So, please, think twice before you break these rules; mull them over; debate them with your friends – I am not insulted.

There are exceptions to all the rules of travel, but you will have to discover them yourself. My goal is to make you a traveler, a thinker, savvy, someone who thinks twice before crossing the planet. Start by reading these rules of travel.

And, yes, sometimes these rules are contradictory, confusing, and lack consistency. Congruence is not my goal. I wrote them to optimize the conditions of your journeys. Travel is uncomfortable, it is not home, and it outside what is normal.

Old maps used to have a warning for travelers at their edges, at the ends of the Earth: "There be dragons." I know these dragons, up close and personal. They share one name, Confusion. So remember these rules as you travel to the edges of our planet and avoid those dragons. ...

This is *real* travel, not a game. The reader, the world traveler, and the casual tourist should all think, ask questions, and above all, find their own paths. This is my goal: to keep you thinking, alert, and questioning the rules. Blindly accepting the rules means you are not thinking, and discovering problems with the rules will train you to travel.

The savvy traveler will instantly think of the exceptions, with stories and examples contrary to the rules. Perfect, consistent, unchallengeable rules would endanger you: You would relax your mind and stop thinking. Please stay alert, look both ways, and think both ways. There is always a better path to follow.

Discover why these rules exist, and you will become a traveler. Ignore them at your own risk.

Although I have circled the planet over 20 times, seen 90 countries, and traveled non-stop for over 16 years, I follow these rules of travel because I learned them the hard way. With this book, you can learn them the easy way.

There is a website called "TheRulesOfTravel.com." People who purchased this book will be able to read the rules online anywhere on the planet using the Internet. You will never be alone; the rules are here to protect you.

God Speed,
Andy Lee Graham

# The Rules ...

# 1. ATM, Bank Money Machine

Experienced travelers stopped carrying traveler checks over 10 years ago. The ATM card is the standard way world travelers get cash from banks.

Following are the rules for using an ATM, with a focus on international travel. Experienced travelers know that ATMs "eat" bank cards.

Imagine only having one ATM card. It is Saturday, the bank is closed, the ATM just ate your card, and your flight leaves on Sunday. You are standing in the street baffled, alone, with no money in a foreign country. This is a real and present problem; this does happens to many travelers abroad.

Clever criminals know that people who just finished using the ATM are easy marks. They watch you; you are guaranteed money, an easy victim. Often, we carry a month's local wages in our hands.

## Non-Negotiable Rules for the ATM, Bank Money Machine

1.  Never make more than two attempts to receive cash. This is when the machine will eat the card, and it is possible your bank at home will deactivate the card. These are protections implemented by banks, but they can also work against you if you are not careful.

2. Never guess your ATM PIN (personal identification number). You either know it, or you do not. And if you are going to guess, only try two times in one session, and only one time per day per machine. It is debatable how many times you can try per day, but the solution is to never guess: Know your PIN number.

3. Do not walk home. When you can, take a taxi. Remember: Criminals want an easy mark. They need a window of time when you are alone to mug you. Another option is to walk home with friends.

4. Do not go to the ATM machine after sunset.

5. Point your back directly at the person behind you so he or she cannot do "shoulder surfing" and see your PIN or bank information, such as your balance.

6. Carry two ATM cards from separate banks.

7. Store your two ATM cards in separate locations in your room. And do not carry them with you when you are out walking around.

8. Do not use third-party, non-bank machines, such as the stand-alone machines they are putting in gas stations, convenience stores, etc. If this type of machine does eat your card, it will be almost hopeless for you retrieve it quickly

9. Take out the maximum amount of money. The international fees are very high, and you do not want to risk using the ATM too often. You need to know the limit at your home bank and the limit locally.

10. Use only machines in front of an actual bank during business hours. If, for any reason, the machine does eat the card, you can retrieve it with the bank staff's help.

It is always better to use a bank's ATM – at a bank – in case it eats your card.

11. Do not use an ATM that feels or looks the least bit strange. If it is broken, damaged, too rough, or the doors are broken, do not use it.

12. Do not count your money at the machine. What are you going to do if it is wrong? If you want to count it, count it inside the bank or at home. Thieves love it when they, too, can count your money, maybe even grab it from your hand.

## Should-Be-Non-Negotiable Rules for the ATM, Bank Money Machine

Swipe Machine -- that does not take card inside!!!!!

Look for Diebold brand, it appears to be best.

13. Go to bank and return directly home.

14. The best time to use the ATM is 10-11 a.m. The machine has been serviced by the bank, and the criminals have not yet arrived.

15. Watch a person in front of you use the ATM successfully so that you can guarantee the machine is tested and working properly.

## Advisable Rules for the ATM, Bank Money Machine

16. Store ATM cards in same locations in your room every time. Most cards are misplaced, lost, and forgotten when people cannot remember where they hid them.

17. Do not hide your ATM cards under the bed for any reason. Hide them in clothing or other places that are guaranteed to be packed again so that you cannot accidentally leave them behind when you move on.

18. If the ATM runs or makes a noise as if you are receiving money, but you are not, stop using the machine. Then, go check your bank account online immediately. If indeed the

money has been taken from your account, you can call the bank, and they will audit and credit your account.

19. ATM machines are safer than walking into a bank for a cash advance on your card.

**Go online to add more rules or corrections to this topic; we will credit you in future additions. TheRulesofTravel.com/1**

# 2. Avoiding Street Attacks

These rules of travel are to help stop us from being physically attacked by locals of a country, but not, however, as the result of attempted robbery, muggings, or criminal behavior. Rather, these are to avoid times where we have somehow aggravated the locals to attack us, accidentally provoked their anger.

Often travelers have identity confusion. We travel the world as if everyone we meet is a foreigner, as if the people living abroad are the aliens. We do not realize that the minute we leave our own country, customs, and cultures, we are often transformed into barbarians. The term "barbarian" refers to a person who is perceived to be uncivilized, one who does not have respect. This accidental, often arrogant contempt for other cultures is dangerous and can result in a tourist being physically attacked. Many tourists have stones thrown at them, as if he or she is a dog.

These rules are to explain common ignorance, arrogance, apathy, and assumptions that endanger tourists and travelers as the foreigners, the aliens, the barbarians that arrive in new countries.

Tourists from rich, developed countries are not granted a reprieve from obeying locals' customs. We are the aliens.

## Non-Negotiable Travel Rules for Avoiding Street Attacks

1. Always have a plausible reason to be visiting a community. Clarity is comforting to people. Cynical remarks or replies, as if there is no reason needed or it is none of the locals' business, are dangerous.

2. Do not walk around intoxicated or sober between 11 p.m. and sunrise.

Do not drink and walk late at night!

3. Never trust religious people. They often believe they are morally superior, but this is contemptuous behavior. Scoundrels are safer, more transparent, and easier to judge, while the religious often entrap you. This is not saying religions are bad; it is saying that the customs of foreign religious people are extremely confusing. Do not trust them or assume you understand them.

Do no associate with armed people.

4.      Do not associate or walk with people who have weapons, whether guns, knives, or other weapons. Weapons scare people, and they will attack you with great force; weapons are an invitation to be attacked. If you feel you need weapons, then leave the area. Staying is agreeing to be attacked.

5.      Assume the police will never come to help, that they do not exist. If you are aware of this, when your bad manners becomes a danger, you realize a small bar fight could be your death.

6.    Enter crowds of people. Crowds deter physical attack, yet are more likely to have pickpockets. When you are in a crowd, the locals cannot focus on you or isolate you from the crowd.

7.    Do not offer money to locals as a way to be forgiven. It is telling people they are for sale; this is an insult. If they ask for money, that is different.

8.    Talking with people who are drinking alcohol or beer is dangerous.

9. Listen for tone of voice that indicates mocking. If you hear this in the voice of locals, then walk away; never discuss or ask why they are mocking you.

10. Avoid protesters with signs, banners, or slogans. Do not try to understand directly from the people involved in the protest why there is a protest. People protest because they are angry; you would be talking with angry people.

Avoid street protests.

11. Do not ignore people. Glance at them and allow them to know you are aware they exist.

12. Before talking to a man or woman, see if there is a person standing waiting for that person. You must be respectful to the group. Being respectful to one person while ignoring the person's girlfriend, boyfriend, husband, wife, or good friend is insulting.

13. If you believe you are about to be attacked, stop and buy food or start playing with kids or gawking at girls.

14. You cannot learn to be safe from people who were attacked multiple times with weapons; they know nothing about staying safe. You learn from people who have obviously been in

dangerous situations where nothing happened. These people managed the situation correctly.

15. Learn the faces of anger and contempt; study body language.

## Advisable Travel Rules for Avoiding Street Attacks

16. Do not be the first to talk. Wait until the locals have greeted you and asked their questions. Talking often is an indication of social status. To be conservative, it is better to allow the locals to talk first. Yet it is better for us to talk loudly with honest and happy body language.

17. Take photos without a hint of shame. If you are feeling nervous or not sure of your welcome, and then do not take a photo.

18. Avoid extremely rich people. They often have unlimited contempt.

19. Always be respectful of stupid behavior. Disrespect, or making a decision that something is stupid, dumb, or simple, is insulting.

20. Do not take photos of police.

21. Avoid loud voices, loud talking, or any sounds that are rising in volume. Often, tourists run right into danger.

22. As you walk, look from left to right, observing the area, making sure you seldom look straight ahead as if you are unaware. People who attack are bullies; they are looking for weakness.

**Go online to add more rules or corrections to this topic; we will credit you in future additions. TheRulesofTravel.com/2**

# 3. Beggars

Observing how people give or refuse to give to beggars is a spiritual enlightenment impossible to avoid as world travelers. Tourist destinations attract beggars. While the locals often know who really needs help and who does not, the tourists cannot know, and, therefore, beggars love tourists.

Beggars create emotional pressure and confusion in people. The beggar wants you to succumb to your emotions and buy your freedom by giving him or her money.

One caution: By giving money, food, or charity, we often feel special. This is power, an elixir that is addictive. People love power. Please, take care and do not become drunk with the power of giving.

The best of us never tell when we give, because telling others grants us power and removes the nobility of giving.

As a rule of thumb, the World Bank defines poverty as earning below 1.25 USD per day, which means that begging can be highly profitable.

Please, as a word of caution: If you know a person who becomes exceptionally angry at beggars, hostile, and sometimes violent, please help this person to walk away immediately from beggars. Maybe returning home is best.

First things first: Who is qualified to receive money?

**Missing Body Parts –** They do not have or are missing body parts, such as an arm, leg, or some other part.

**Too Old to Work –** There are very old people with no money. This is 100 percent the responsibility of the country. But I do give very old people money because it is an immediate problem. But be wary: There are some clever old beggars who beg as a career choice.

Legless beggars in Niger

**Food Beggars –** I am not talking about money. Say you have a piece of bread in your hands, and a person looks at you and wants you to share it, to give him or her some, then it is probably best to share.

**Special Crazy –** There are those people that are so crazy that they do not know how to take care of themselves. I saw a guy in Otavalo, Ecuador, who was in shorts, freezing, and sitting on the sidewalk. I saw this man daily, and he never asked for money or food. I gave him some food. I am not sure he would know what to do with money.

**Maimed on Purpose –** I am told that in some places the people cripple or maim their children on purpose. I would not give to these cripples. It would only make them do it to another and another and another. But think on this one; tell me your ideas. Obviously, giving to these beggars is a personal decision, and in many ways, they are special crazy.

## Non-Negotiable Travel Rules for Beggars

1. Begging would end if nobody would give.

2. Do not give to beggars until you know why.

3. Do not give to beggars until you have been in the country for 30 days and understand the localized beggar situation.

4. Admit to yourself that you want the beggars to leave.

5. We pay beggars to leave.

6. You are not responsible for beggars.

7. Admit to yourself that beggars are annoying.

8. Do not refuse people begging for bread.

9. The beggar you give to today will find you tomorrow.

10. Do not make begging profitable, never more than 1.25 USD per day.

11. Offer beggars jobs when possible.

12. If a local is giving, then maybe you can give.

13. Beggars are not nice people who have problems.

14. Beggars seldom get jobs.

15. Inspect the beggar for missing body parts.

16. Giving money encourages begging.

17. Learn why you feel responsible, guilty, or angry.

18. Do not give to beggar near your home or hotel.

19. Do not talk with beggars. Give, but never talk.

If you give, give a lot, not a little. Feed a girl like this for a day, at least.

20. Make jobs, not beggars

21. Do not enable beggars to thrive.

22. Give a lot, not a little, to beggars, enough for one day.

23. We give to beggars to relieve guilt, not to help them.

24. Do not give money to people that do not ask for money. That is an insult.

25. Do not give to OBNOXIOUS beggars.

26. Do not do the job of the government.

27. Do not give to beggars who enter restaurants.

28. Do not trust a beggar.

**Go online to add more rules or corrections to this topic; we will credit you in future additions. TheRulesofTravel.com/3**

# 4. Budgeting

In the last 15 years of my perpetual travels, I have slowly realized that vacations are not times when people wish to budget. People are on holiday from the day-to-day grind of watching what we spend, from prioritizing and planning. Generally, a vacation is a time to splurge, live the life of leisure, and for 1-2 weeks of the year, be as close to the rich and famous as possible.

Saying this, a vacation budget is a contradiction in terms. How can we be on vacation if we have to continually think about money? Few people stay on a travel budget: They are on vacation, and few people enjoy being called cheap. Even the super-rich have an upper limit to spending money.

Is it a hotel, or a hotel, or a joke?

HOTEL
HOSTEL

Lodging will use any word they think your budget wants!
Beware: Home Aways from Home, and Eco-Friendly, or Budget

The topic of travel budgets is infused with angry words; nobody wants to be reminded how they failed daily and how they fell to temptations. We are all human and, therefore, prone to temptations. The hope is to remove the temptations yet enjoy life.

## Non-Negotiable Travel Rules for Budgeting

1.   The destination country and hotel determine our travel budget.

2. The faster your travel, the more expensive.

3. Cash and credit cards in a traveler's pocket are used. They enable us to fall to temptations and buy things we later regret.

4. Leave your credit cards and large cash in your hotel room.

5. Know your daily travel budget number.

6. Choosing a hotel you can afford is the best budget.

7. Fly to the cheap countries first.

8. Nobody wants to budget for travel, but it is required.

9. Everyone has a budget – some are larger.

10. People who stay on travel budget are called cheap.

11. All-inclusive resorts make travel budgets easy.

12. You know you are on budget when people call you cheap. The tourist industry thrives because people refuse to be called cheap. It is an insult given by people who are contemptuous and have no respect for you. This this is not the same as a "Cheap Charlie" who wants 10 dollars' worth of value and will lie so he or she can pay 3 dollars.

13. The enemy of a budget is ready-to-use cash.

14. Do not pay if confused.

15. Do not sign on a contract the first day.

16.  People return home when they run out of money.

## Advisable Travel Rules for Budgeting

17.  To travel on a budget, you need to be able to run out of money.

18.  Estimate the amount of time it takes to work to buy something. For example, if I earn 10 dollars per hour, it takes 30 minutes to buy a 5 dollar hamburger.

19.  Do not enter places you cannot afford with pocket money.

20.  Carry only your daily budget

21.  Count how much money is left to spend. Counting money spent is of no value.

22.  Traveling to countries you cannot afford makes for a miserable trip.

23.  Running out of money means you have hit your maximum budget.

24.  Travel writing in paper books tells the truth, and Internet writers lie.

25.  Always ask and know the exact price before you buy.

26.  Carry a specific amount of cash daily in your pocket to spend. And when going over budget, use credit cards while always

remembering that using credit cards abroad quadruples your chance of identity theft.

27. Know the price of a taxi before you enter.

28. Worry when you hear the words, budget, cheap, honest, value, eco-friendly, or any words you *want* to hear. When something is really cheap and a good value, then people are lined up waiting to use or purchase it. Hotels that are 100 percent full generally are worth the money.

29. The tourist industry wants you believe duty free shops are cheap.

30. Never say, "But it was so cheap, I could not resist." These are the words of a person who regularly justifies going over-budget, and to savvy travelers, it makes you appear foolish, and it makes you a target of unscrupulous people. …

31. Write the excuses you used to go over budget down, and then throw the paper away. This will help you to remember. However, there is no reason to sit around worried all day.

32. People believe they can say no to temptations.

**Go online to add more rules or corrections to this topic; we will credit you in future additions. TheRulesofTravel.com/4**

# 5. Business Hotel Rooms

The goal of business travel is to work, and the hotel serves as a temporary office. Our business hotel or any five-star hotel needs to have the listed benefits in the room. Our goal as business travelers is to live identically or better than at home.

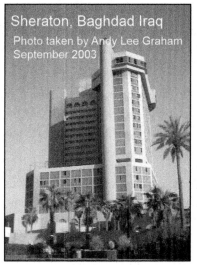

Sheraton, Baghdad Iraq
Photo taken by Andy Lee Graham
September 2003

Good employers realize that travel is uncomfortable and expensive. Wise employers often require employees to stay in specific hotel chains, which provide these benefits, so that there is no confusion, no need to adapt to strange environments.

Many business people choose airlines because of frequent flyer points and hotels that are fun. Employers can view this as a bonus to workers.

These rules are the minimal requirements of business hotel or any five-star hotel on the planet. If they are not provided, the hotel is not ready for business travelers, or the traveler does not wish to work in the hotel room.

I have lived in over 1,000 hotels in 90 countries. I am a business person who has run an Internet business now for 13 years while continuously traveling the planet.

## Non-Negotiable Travel Rules for Hotel Rooms for Business

1. There are 1-3 electrical plugs on each wall of the hotel room.

2. There is a desk with pens and notepaper.

3. There is laundry drop-off in the morning at reception and pickup in the afternoon. This is a good test question: Call up a prospective business hotel and ask whether this is provided. The answer will be revealing

4. There is good lighting for reading in bed and at the desk. When the desk light is turned on, it does not annoy one's bed partner.

5. There is room service serving food and drinks from 5 a.m. until midnight. The best business hotels provide 24-hour service because international airline flights leave 24 hours per day. Eating in the business hotel room allows the traveler to avoid adapting to locals' customs. And, he or she can order room service before taking a shower and have the food waiting, thereby using time more effectively.

6. There should be a telephone in the room for local or international calls. It is a myth that your cell phone will work in all countries; this is still not possible.

7. There should be a fax machine on the property for 24-hour reception and sending of faxes.

8. Wi-Fi should be provided in all areas of the hotel for free, and in the room there should be an Ethernet wire as an alternate way to connect when concrete walls weaken the Wi-Fi signal. Business travelers have

clients meet them at the hotel, and both parties need to have Internet access. Additional hotel charges for connections works against the goal of the business traveler, which is to enter the room and start working immediately.

9. The hotel receptionist knows the price of taxis for a daily rate and can have a taxi arrive in less than 15 minutes. Business travelers often spend hours reading maps in rental cars, when their time would be better used working and allowing the driver to find locations. Drivers are safer for the business traveler as they keep people from accidentally driving a rental car into dangerous neighborhoods.

10. Business travelers need a bellman or porter to run errands.

11. There should be private office rooms off the lobby area where business travelers can meet clients.

## Advisable Travel Rules for Hotel Rooms for Business

Hotel receptionist, Lima, Peru

12. The receptionist should speak adequate English; this is the language of business worldwide.

13. Public libraries in the USA make great meeting places.

14. There are typing services available to assist with business documents.

15. The hotel has one purchased Internet connection for every 5-10 guests. In hotels over 300 USD per night, the connection should not be shared with other guests.

**Go online to add more rules or corrections to this topic; we will credit you in future additions. TheRulesofTravel.com/5**

# 6. Clothing

Traveling the planet is similar to going on a job interview that never ends.

Some of us will thrive as international travelers and never return home. But others fail to adapt because they fail to accept that travel is an inherently uncomfortable experience, both for us and the locals we meet abroad.

Photographer with the right clothes for the job

Choose the correct clothing, which makes you feel smart, safe, and secure enough to travel in comfort.

To be comfortable, travelers need to know that their money is in their pockets and that their camera or their iPad cannot easily be stolen. If you are not relaxed and comfortable, that is your subconscious mind telling you there are problems.

Your clothing, body language, and spoken words are the bundle of characteristics that defines who you are. We can change our clothing, but to erase a lifetime of culture is not possible. And as travelers, we speak first with clothing.

To locals who do not speak our language, our clothing and body language are how they judge us. Whether you are safe, stupid, smart, clever, or naïve, the clothing is half the interview; therefore, we need to dress for travel success.

There are travelers who spend days buying special clothing, as if the people in the country they will visit do not wear clothing and it will be impossible to buy anything. They sell clothing in all countries on the planet.

Travel is the art of fitting in everywhere, as if you lived in a place all your life. To be called a "tourist" means you lose. When people believe you live in that place, then you win.

## Non-Negotiable Travel Rules for Clothing

1.  Know which set of clothing you will wear to dinner with an ambassador. Many times, we are invited to visit extremely rich and important people. Do you have the clothing to wear? In small countries, we can often meet important embassy workers. I carry khaki pants and all-white gym shoes, as well as a collared shirt.

2.  Do not wear clothing with metal sewn onto the clothing to the airport. Airport security will need to pull you aside and search your body, and it will take longer to pass through, delaying the line.

3.  Wear the same set of clothing for every long-haul trip. Choose a set of clothing that is optimized for comfort, safety, and

storage, and that will go through airport security. There is nothing more uncomfortable than having the wrong clothing on a 22-hour plane flight … or 30 hours when delayed. Sleeping in airports is common, and elastic in clothing cuts into your skin. Cargo pants are especially valuable for airports; you can carry 10 pounds of gear in the pockets when needed.

4. Things that can fall out of your pockets *will* fall out of your pockets.

5. Know where and how you will carry your money belt or neck pouch, or have special secret pockets sewn into all clothing you wear.

6. Obese people will have trouble buying clothes overseas. Take extra care making sure you have too much clothing and not too little.

7. Buy men's underwear at home. It is difficult to buy in over 200 countries on the planet.

8. Wear shoes that are easy to remove when visiting homes of local people. Many people prefer you remove your shoes to enter their home.

9. Do not wear dirty clothing; the general public believes these people are stupid and easier to rob.

10. Experienced travelers modify their clothing. Beware of advice from travelers who have never taken clothing to tailors to modify and adapt for travel.

11. It is better to leave with too much underwear and bras, then throw them away later. But you can under-pack other clothes and buy them at your destination.

12. You will not be allowed to wear military camouflage clothing in some countries.

13. Pack a swimsuit. There are times when you need to use a public shower or the whole tour group goes to the hot tub. One time, I needed to buy a swimsuit at a snow ski resort. And entering a shower house in China is embarrassing. Often tourists receive oil, or wet or body massages where it is best to have the minimal amount of clothing on – or none.

14. Safe pockets are difficult to open; easy-to-open pockets are easy to pickpocket.

15. When there is a choice between a shirt with a collar or no collar, choose the shirt with no collar. It takes up less space, and collars are difficult to clean and take longer to dry on a clothes line.

"In Uniform" at: Machu Picchu, Peru

16. Hunting vests with many pockets allow a traveler to carry another 10-30 pounds onto the plane.

17. Do not wear clothing that makes you look like a tourist. Even though we travelers are tourists, looking like tourists makes us

a target for crime. Tourists generally have more valuables with them and are more confused than the locals; therefore, they are easy targets.

18. Seductive clothing on women in many countries means you are easy to take to bed, or a slut, or worse.

19. Travel pants do not have elastic waistbands. Elastic will slowly cut off circulation and make you feel uncomfortable.

20. Wear belts with plastic buckles, and you will go through airport detectors more quickly.

21. Wear clothing that you love, that makes you feel confident and happy. Do not wear dark clothing because it does not show dirt; you'll be tempted to wear dirty, smelly clothing, which is a great way to lose friends.

22. Going native – wearing all the clothing of a destination country – means the traveler is inexperienced. Packed clothing from 10-20 countries means the person is experienced. People in destination countries like us to wear a few items of their clothing, but to wear a full outfit means we will be called crazy.

23. Know what to carry with you in your clothing, then choose the clothing that allows you to carry these items.

24. If you are dressing radically different than other people, expect to be treated radically different. Barbaric behavior is when you disobey the local customs and culture of a country.

25. Do not buy hiking clothing to travel – Are you going on trip or trekking? Travel clothing stops pickpockets and thieves, and hiking clothing allows easy access to thieves.

26. Do not buy travel clothing; buy clothing qualified for travel. Generally, manufactures of clothes describe their clothing as anything that sells clothing. I have never purchased any clothing made for travel.

27. Do not carry irreplaceable, important family clothing.

28. If you can put your hands in the pockets easily, so can a pickpocket.

29. Buttons are safer than Velcro, and Velcro is better than nothing over the pockets for protection from thieves.

30. Ask your friends, "Do I look like a tourist?" If the answer is yes, then get help dressing.

## Advisable Travel Rules for Clothing

31. Do not worry about forgetting clothing; you can buy clothing in every country on the planet.

32. 80-90 percent of the travel clothing sold is seriously flawed in design; generally, manufacturers are selling hiking clothing for plane, train, and bus trips. The designers of clothing are marketing experts, not travelers, and they know that people buy fashions and gimmicks.

33. Carry enough clothing to layer for winter weather, enough to stay warm.

34. Weigh your clothing at the delicatessen, post office, or a shipping center.

35. Wear clothing that has two layers of cloth between your valuables and a knife. Many pickpockets use a knife or razorblade to cut out your wallet or valuables as they pass.

36. Choose the clothing that stops theft.

37. The clothing does not work if you need to remove items from your pockets to sit down. Say you have a very large cell phone, and you remove it to put it on the table. I guarantee a day will come when you forget it or the phone is stolen.

38. If you carry a piece of clothing for longer than three months on an around-the-world trip and never wear it, give or throw it in the trash.

39. The best place to buy underwear, panties, and socks is in your home country.

40. People buy clothing as souvenirs; therefore, pack less clothing than you need.

41. The best place to buy clothing in the 200 poor countries is in second-hand stores. It is difficult to buy normal clothing in these countries, but second-hand stores have designer clothing cheap.

42. Your hotel seldom has enough clothes hangers in closets; carry or buy some when possible.

43. Mailing or shipping clothing to a destination is often cheaper.

44. Velcro cargo pockets are easy to pickpocket.

45. Carry a sweatshirt or light jacket on around-the-world trips.

46. Do not wear shorts on overnight buses, planes, or trains. Many times, the air conditioning is too cold for comfort.

47. Pockets that twist inside are best.

48. Travel pants with removable legs telegraph to criminals that you are a tourist.

49. Long-sleeved shirts are needed for heavily mosquito-infested areas.

50. The string at the bottom of army pants is to stop mosquitoes from entering.

51. Try to keep all the colors in one load of laundry. If you can wash all your clothing in one load, it is cheaper.

**Go online to add more rules or corrections to this topic; we will credit you in future additions. TheRulesofTravel.com/6**

# 7. Cooling Tropical Hotel Rooms

Every person on the planet would die in less than 5 minutes without air to breath; oxygen is the most essential need of humans.

And, often, we also believe "We cannot live without air conditioning!"

In reality, we thrive without air-con!

Living in over 1,000 hotel rooms has forced me to accept that to truly feel better, I should breathe normal air, neither heated nor cooled. Today, and for the rest of my life, I will continue to seek places to live where there is no need for furnaces or air conditioning.

The rules below will help you find the type of room, whether a hotel, apartment, or house, that does not require unnatural conditioning of air. Following these rules and living naturally will allow us to avoid paying 100-300 USD per month in electric bills. That is just a little bit more that we can stop working for money and enjoy life instead.

As savvy travelers know, we can choose to live in dwellings that optimize our relationship with the sun, wind, and water.

For example, a concrete building that has wind coming from the ocean, yet which is far enough away from it, will have dry, humidity-free air. This naturally cool air will blow freely through the building, granting us a fresh, cool breeze. Add to that tall shade trees that block direct sunlight from beating on the windows, roof, or near our room, and we have a lovely, comfortable home – AC not needed.

## Non-Negotiable Travel Rules for Cooling Your Tropical Hotel Room

1. Do not live in buildings with steel roofs because the sun beats on the roof and turns your room into an oven.

2. Rent rooms with one full story of concrete hotel rooms above your room. This floor of concrete will insulate you from the heat. Be warned: This can also work against you. If there is no shade on the outside of the building and the average temperature rises, all that concrete will retain heat. But the general rule is that you want to live in a concrete cave with plenty of concrete as a heat barrier.

First and second story kept cooler by concrete top story

3. Never tolerate or make due with a hot room. Move to another room inside the hotel until you are comfortable, or change hotels. Live the life of leisure, comfort; toleration of discomfort is not the lifestyle we chose. This is one reason to never reserve a room: You can

change hotels without penalty if your first choice does not have a comfortable room.

4. There must be a way to create cross-ventilation in the room, where the air enters into the room from one location and exits through another. Hot air rises; the goal is to keep this hot air out of the room and keep humidity off the concrete walls.

5. Change the sheets often to ensure they are dry, clean, and smelling fresh.

6. Rent rooms that remain cool with or without air conditioning. If the only way it stays cool is AC, then one electrical outage will turn the room into a sauna. If you have zero choice about using AC, then this is a major design problem with the hotel.

7. Turn incandescent light bulbs off when not in use; they give off a lot of heat. Compact fluorescent or LED lights give off little or no heat.

8. Take off your clothes when you enter your hotel room. This saves on cleaning clothes and allows your skin to ventilate. I have a special towel that has a pull cord, which I wear in the room, or a pair of light shorts.

9.    Do not rent rooms where the sun shines directly into the room for half the day. If there is a balcony or awning over the window, it alleviates 50 percent of the room's greenhouse effect. Seeing the sunrise or sunset from your window is not a benefit: It means your hotel room has the greenhouse effect.

10. Rent a room with a floor fan. Ceiling fans do not create proper cross-ventilation, and you cannot adjust the direction to keep the wind out of your eyes.

11. At night, have the floor fan rotated to point over the foot of the bed and out the window. When the fan is strategically located, you can use one fan to both service your bed and to blow stale air out of the room.

12. Keep the restroom door closed whenever possible to keep water from evaporating into your living quarters and causing the humidity to rise. Note: If you are going to build a shower or restroom in a house, truly make it outside the dwelling areas.

13. Close curtains during the day to keep the sun from shining in, and open them wide at night to allow cooler air to enter.

14. Do not make do with only the hotel fan; buy an extra if hot.

15. Do not conserve electricity; leave the fan running with the intention of making the stale air blow out the window.

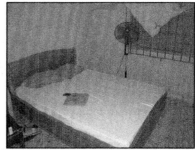

16. Stop any smells by wiping down surfaces with chlorine (bleach) and water to remove any oils. Somehow, a disinfected room feels cooler.

Position fan for maximum ventilation

17. Take showers often to keep all smells and oils off your body.

18. Change your shirt 2-4 times per day. When the least bit of perspiration is on your shirt, it is time to change it. Note: when in the room, remember to remove your clothing.

## Advisable Travel Rules for Cooling Your Tropical Hotel Room

19. Do not have a refrigerator in your room. The heat coming off a fridge is overbearing.

20. Do not have a hot water heater inside the room. It should be outside the room so that the excess heat dissipates outside. On-demand electrical or propane hot water heaters are ideal for a hotel.

21. Respect a hotel that believes in shade trees. This is the difference between a parking lot hotel and a garden hotel.

22. Attic spaces above your room need to have roof vents to allow hot air to escape. If the place is super, there will be an electric fan blowing the air out of this dead air space.

23. Cook outside enclosed rooms in the open air. Having a kitchen in your enclosed house is sort of silly. The locals generally have an open-air kitchen, not one inside the house.

24. Keep the toilet lid down so water evaporation does not increase room humidity.

25. Dry clothing outside the room when possible.

**Go online to add more rules or corrections to this topic; we will credit you in future additions. TheRulesofTravel.com/7**

# 8. Doctors

Tourists and fellow travelers comment about doctors, medical facilities, and medicines as if foreign countries are other planets. Often, comments border on racism, as if one race, maybe the American or German, is exclusively intelligent.

The primary difference between overseas medical care and that of home is the machines, the testing, and the analysis. If they have good medical equipment, then even the worst of doctors often can find solutions to difficult problems.

I have a friend who is a doctor, and I can send him medical reports

and get some opinions for free. He is not going to charge me (or admit he does this), and he gives me many lectures.

I, Andy Lee Graham, paid 120 USD for an MRI in the Philippines to diagnose sciatica. I regularly have x-rays done on a broken femur, and they are stored as digital files. I pay 3-10 USD per x-ray.

The best way to use doctors abroad is for prevention. In 200 countries, we can afford

Dancing doctor, Guatemala

to ask questions and prevent health problems. That alone makes traveling abroad to talk to doctors worth it.

I prefer the Philippines because they have American veterans' hospitals, which have English-speaking staff and are certified for veterans from the USA. I can pay 10 USD per doctor visit – This is Doctor Paradise.

## Non-Negotiable Travel Rules for Doctors

1.  Doctors in foreign countries try to advertise to cheat tourists. They will charge tourists in private hospitals 10 times the cost of normal public hospitals. You can visit the same doctor in the public hospital.

2.  We can find doctors as smart as American doctors overseas. Many doctors inside the USA are from India, Ghana, and other countries, yet their peers in their home countries are just as smart. If you believe this cannot be true, then do not go to a doctor in the USA who was born abroad.

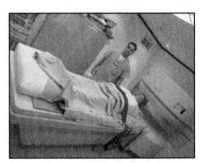
Me, getting an MRI in the Philippines

3.  It is possible to become as smart as a doctor about one specific medical problem. With the Internet, the entire world's

information is at our fingertips. (It is possible, but that does not mean you have the brain.)

4. Pharmacies serve as doctors in 200 countries. These countries still have doctors, but primary medical assistance is done in the pharmacy.

5. In many countries, the doctor is free but the medicines cost.

6. Good machines, laboratories, and medicine make the doctor. Funny: Yes, Cuba may have good doctors, but they do not have adequate equipment or medicines after they diagnose the problem.

7. Ask the doctor how much the fee is before you enter.

## Advisable Travel Rules for Doctors

8. Go to the laboratories first and bypass the doctor.

9. You can be your own doctor: Medicine and laboratory services in 200 countries are available to laymen.

10. Diagnose the disease in the USA and have it treated abroad.

**Go online to add more rules or corrections to this topic; we will credit you in future additions. TheRulesofTravel.com/8**

# 9. Electrical Power Adapters

These rules are written for a people who need electricity daily for 3-5 electrical devices and want to travel anywhere and everywhere on the planet. This is for travelers who leave the resorts and the five-star hotels, and who live with the locals.

## Typical List of Travelers' Electrical Devices

- Cell phone

- Smart phone or tablet

- Computer

## Other Electrical Travelers' Devices

- **Wall lamp/light** – I recommend book readers carry a portable, plug-in-the wall light if they wish to read daily because hotels seldom provide the minimal amount of light to read in bed.

- **Hot plate** – For the budget traveler, carrying an electrical hot plate can save thousands of dollars per year.

## Worst Case Scenarios for Electricity

This is a room that only has one florescent light fixture, and the village turns on the gas-powered generator for 1-4 hours just after sunset.

Another bad situation is a hostel in Europe. These often have 10 cell phones plugged into one electrical outlet.

## Non-Negotiable Travel Rules for Electrical Power Adapters

1. Do not accept electrical problems; if you plan to travel for years, then do not live with inadequate electrical access. Putting

Universal adapters

up with less than what you truly want and desire is one of the primary reasons people stop traveling. Living in mild discomfort for years because you do not wish to carry an extension cord, a room light, or just walk into a hardware store to buy a splitter is the part of the bundle of discomforts that lead one to stop traveling the planet.

2. To have electricity 100 percent of the time, stay in five-star chain hotels, such as Hyatt and Sheraton. Business hotels are usually equipped with universal electrical power adapters. Do

not stay in trendy or highly recommended hotels; you must stay in the major chains. Boutique hotels and bed and breakfasts are problematic.

3.  Do not expect to find adequate electrical outlets in European hostels. The number of outlets is usually inadequate for the number of people in a dormitory.

4.  There is no electrical power adapter sold that will allow you to have electricity in every hotel room on the planet. There are hotel rooms with only one light bulb hanging down in the center of the room, and then you need a two-outlet light bulb socket adapter. In the

Homemade "adapter" using electrical tape and alligator clamps

worst scenario, there is only one florescent light in the room, and you need to splice into the electrical switch by using alligator clips to connect.

5.  For world travel, coordinate electrical power adapters with an extension cord with at least four outlets. Consider when buying electrical adapters: Are you buying an adapter for every electrical device – one for the cell phone, battery charger, computer, tablet, etc.? Or will the extension cord serve as the adapter? (The second option is the smart choice.)

6. Walk around in hardware stores in all countries you visit to learn which types of electrical power adapters are available for sale. If you do not want to enter hardware stores, then you need to stay in five-star, business-traveler-serving hotels to have reliable electricity.

7. Learn basic electrical wiring to have electricity 100 percent of the time. There will be times when you have to cut into the electrical wires, repair the plugs in the hotel room, or use alligator clips to connect directly into a light switch.

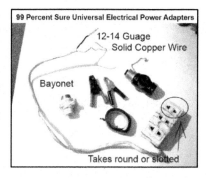

99 Percent Sure Universal Electrical Power Adapters

12-14 Guage Solid Copper Wire

Bayonet

Takes round or slotted

8. Accept that electrical light bulb sockets or florescent light fixtures will sometimes be the only source of electricity in the hotel room.

9. Buy electrical splitters to fit your adapters, a device to make one outlet into three.

## Advisable Travel Rules for Electrical Power Adapters

10. A cold-water shower is a sign of no electricity because the hotel is too cheap to pay for it.

11. Plug electronic devices in plain sight so that you do not forget them when you leave the hotel. Finding replacement adapters is often easier in poorer countries and difficult in expensive countries.

12. Adapters are for your extension cord, not the wall outlets. Devices work best using the plug of your native country.

13. The one adapter you use daily will be forgotten, left in the hotel, so you need to buy two when they are not easy to find. Sometimes, hardware stores will not normally stock the right adapters in your present country.

14. Do not use adapters in electrical plug outlets that are so old, loose, and sloppy that your adapter falls out. This is an unsafe electrical connection for your electronic devices.

15. Do not worry about electricity if you are staying in hotels; there is always a way to plug in your electronic devices. You may need to plug them in at the reception desk or the owner's apartment, but there is a way.

16. Do not put more than one adapter in sequence because doing so can make the adapters burn up or the electricity arc.

17. An extension cord is more important than an adapter.


**Go online to add more rules or corrections to this topic; we will credit you in future additions. TheRulesofTravel.com/9**

# 10. Hotels (General Advice)

Hotels are uncomfortable – unless you are homeless.

Humans have a hierarchy of needs, and we are never happy and content until our basic needs are met. To be happy in a hotel, a person has to live better than at home or accept that being uncomfortable is the natural feeling of travel.

Typical U.S. $0-5 hotel room

It is natural for humans to complain about hotels. People diligently try to accept and make the best of their temporary homes. Herein is the challenge of staying in hotels: We believe we need to make the best of our temporary home, but we are uncomfortable until we make a home a home. But in the end, it is a hotel, so we complain when it is not home.

The word, "hotel," is the common man's name for all forms of lodging or accommodation. People say, "I am going back to the hotel." It does not matter if we are in a hostel, family home, or five-star hotel with an oceanfront view: We think "hotel," and we say "hotel." Resorts are different from our hotels.

There are no explanations below for the rules. We want you to dwell, muse, and derive your best personal reasons for why these rules make sense.

**Remember:** Know these hotel travel rules before you break them!

## Non-Negotiable Travel Rules for Hotels

1. Enjoy the stupidity of hotels.

2. Expect a reception at a hotel.

3. Sleep in the best room of the hotel.

4. The destination is more important than the hotel.

5. Sleep in safe hotels.

6. Pay daily in the morning to same hotel staff member.

7. Get a receipt for your room.

8. Inspect your room before you check in.

9. Breathing is important in hotels.

10. Mosquito nets are in cheap hotels.

Mosquito netting – one sure sign of a cheap hotel

11. Locking a key in your hotel room should not be possible.

12. When asked, "When will you return to your room?" say, "In a few minutes." Never say to the reception desk that you will be gone all day. This would telegraph to the staff your room is available for many hours of theft.

## Advisable Travel Rules for Hotels

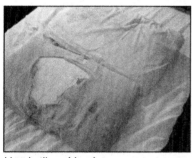
Hotel pillow, Nepal

13.  Do not stay in hotels that require you to drive a car.

14.  Public transportation should reach the hotel.

15.  Check the hot water.

16.  Reading lights in hotels are handy.

Every once in a while, to truly enjoy the stupidity of hotels, take the pillow cases and sheets off the bed.

Or, for kicks and giggles, jump onto the bed to see if the sheets survive.

We hunt for our basic needs in hotels, and we need to remember the hotel paradox: In our traveler's mind, we are trying to accept the hotel as an uncomfortable home, but a hotel is never a home.

**Go online to add more rules or corrections to this topic; we will credit you in future additions. TheRulesofTravel.com/10**

# 11. Hotels That Are Unacceptable

Living in a hotel room is the same as home ownership: Our hotel room is really our home away from home. So we must apply the same rules as our home to a hotel room. And the management of the hotel must give us our rights as homeowners: no searches, no entry, and good neighbors.

How you live in a hotel is not a review of the hotel. It is a revelation about who you are and how you live.

Please note that dirty, disorganized, and improperly furnished hotel rooms are the cheaper rooms on the planet.

Expect your Hotel to be a home away from home, and you will get the life you deserve.

Hotels are somewhere on a continuum between super clean to outlandishly dirty, and in the final analysis, hotels on the planet are, "what you see is what you get." So we need to inspect a room before we agree to live there. Most hotel rooms can be transformed into top-notch hotels easily if we accept that we are responsible for how we live.

Each hotel room is our new, temporary home, and the rules of home apply, so cleaning and improving the room shows who we are and how we live at home. Many guests enter hotel rooms and treat them differently than their homes, living as brutes. The hotel and the room need to be treated as our home.

Everything on the lists below reveals the personal qualities of the owner, manager, and staff of the hotel.

## Non-Negotiable: These Are Unacceptable Hotels

This list of things includes those we cannot change about a hotel, and by refusing to accept them, we can easily improve the quality of our world travels tenfold.

1. Hotels that allow bad hotel guests, our neighbors, to violate our rights of privacy, quiet, and respect are always unacceptable. This is why a family owned hotel, with the owners living in the hotel, is normally the best choice for world travelers.

2. Management cannot enter a hotel room without your permission. Many hotels believe they have the right to inspect your room when you are away, and this is the way 90 percent of hotel theft occurs. Your room is your home, and your right to privacy and security must not be violated.

3. There must be no cats, dogs, or other pets in common areas of the hotel or capable of entering your room. We assume you do not allow strange dogs and cats to enter your home, and this rule applies in your new home, the hotel room.

4. Hotels that refuse to allow your friends to enter your room are unacceptable. Friends are the most important thing humans have, and to exclude them from entering your room is again a violation of your home rights.

5. Mattresses must not be filthy or have broken springs or holes in them; this is just not worth our time.

6. There should be no mosque or church next door with loud prayers or music.

7. Do not live in hotels with construction project noise.

8. Mold in a room is unacceptable. You cannot clean it yourself; this is not fixable.

## Advisable to Avoid

These are conditions that are changeable. Often, a drastically disgusting room can be transformed into a palace. If you find these conditions exist, it tells you about the values, ethics, lifestyle, and quality of life of the owner and management.

9. Condom under bed or used condoms anywhere in the room.

10. Chewing gum ground into the floor, stuck on the floor, and looking like a round dot on the floor.

11. Dirty toilet seat bottom.

12. Un-flushed toilets.

13. Pillow is dirty – take off the pillowcase and inspect.

14. Bed appears to have had someone sleeping in it, maybe for quick sex, and the bed has not been properly cleaned.

15. Bed spread is sticky. Strangely, there are Middle Eastern and Indian beds where the bedcover is seldom cleaned.

16. Staff urinating in public or near the hotel. This is an indication of the quality of humans you are living with, your new neighbors.

What we can change in a hotel room often makes a hotel cheaper. What we cannot change makes a hotel unacceptable for human dwelling.

The world is self-service, and if we jump in, buy some hangers for the room, supervise the cleaning staff, and realize this is really our home, we can all live like kings and queens.

**Go online to add more rules or corrections to this topic; we will credit you in future additions. TheRulesofTravel.com/11**

# 12. Hotel Windows

The concrete box stops the sun from directly shining into room.

Cannot crimb over.

AC

Very Close to Ideal Hotel Windows

Most tourist hotels have air conditioning, and often guests cannot open the windows. This is easier for the hotel, but conditioned air, which has been cooled or heated, is not paradise. Fresh air is always the best choice. Remember these rules about hotel rooms, and you will always have the hotel room with the best windows.

## Non-Negotiable Rules

1.  People should not be able to walk up to the window, put their hands through the window, and reach inside to unlock the door.

2.  We need at least one window in a hotel room to provide fresh air. Often, people in air-conditioned rooms feel weak and sick.

3.  People walking by our window should not be able to reach in and take things from the room, for example, being able to steal your camera from atop a table by the window.

4.  We need to check the windows to ensure they lock properly or are too small for humans to enter. Open and close the windows, making sure they function properly before agreeing to the hotel room.

5.  There should be no way for a human to enter the room through the windows, whether there are bars on the windows or they are too small for humans.

6.  People should not be able to access and climb through a window from an adjoining balcony or from the roof and enter the room.

Exhaust fan over door provides ventilation without risking security

## Advisable Rules

7.  It is better to not have windows on entrance doors to your hotel. These windows allow in noise, can be broken by thieves to gain access, and are not private.

8.  There should be curtains that will cover the windows and completely block the sunlight. This is rare, yet in fan-only rooms, stopping the sun from entering stops the greenhouse effect from making the room hot.

9. Try to avoid hotel windows that face a common courtyard or atrium because these will allow loud noise to echo through your room. These types of windows need to be soundproof, which is normally a double paned, vacuum-sealed window.

10. When you open a window, there should be cross-flow ventilation in the room; there should be a way for the air to enter and leave. Two facing windows is best for cross flow.

11. We need to check there are screens on windows to protect against mosquitoes that carry dengue, malaria, etc. It would seem to be common sense that this rule should be non-negotiable, yet there are countries where one can seldom find a window with screens, and some of the best hotels in cities do not see screens as necessary.

12. Windows should face the morning sun and not the sunset. This will keep the room cooler and allow you to awaken without an alarm.

13. Shutters on the inside of a room are great because they allow you to stop all the sunlight from entering, and they are great for security.

14. Windows should not be above the desk area because this will allow rain to enter and damage computers. Plus, sunlight on the computer causes glare.

15. The window should allow direct site of you lying in bed.

16. The best window only receives indirect sun, usually because there is a balcony in front or some form of cover that extends out 3-7 feet.

## Great Windows

A.     A great window has a fan in the window that can force air to enter or leave the room, creating good ventilation and making it easy to breathe.

B.     A great window does not allow direct sunlight to enter. There is a canopy over the top of the window or side walls that extend out.

C. A great window has shutters on the inside of the hotel-room window.

**Go online to add more rules or corrections to this topic; we will credit you in future additions. TheRulesofTravel.com/12**

# 13. Hotel Keys

It is amazing how many hotels hang your room key up behind the reception desk, telegraphing to everyone that your room is vacant, that you have left the hotel, and your room is ready to be robbed.

This is your home in a foreign land, where you are a stranger; all your personal possessions are in your temporary home.

## Non-Negotiable Rules for Key Management

1.  You need to know who has extra copies of the hotel room key. When you discover how many people actually have access to your hotel room and just how disorganized the average bed and breakfast, boutique hotel, or mom-and-pop hotels is, you will be scared into obeying the rules of travel.

    Note: a truly good hotel will say, "We have one, but that is none of your business." This happens in about 1 in 200 hotels, and usually the cleaning lady is sent to grab them. ...

2.  Carry keys and not combination locks. It seems smart to have a combination lock until you are standing with your

Keyed luggage locks better than combination locks

luggage outside the hotel, trying to adjust your bifocals to see the lock, and fumbling the little dials.

3. Place an LED flashlight device on your key ring because 90-98 percent of the hotels on the planet do not have lights at your

door. An alternative is to have a flashlight app on your cell phone.

4. If there is a hasp on the door, then use your own padlock; never use the hotel's padlock.

5. Look at the keys in your hand before you pull a hotel room door shut. Often, people have home keys and room keys, and they both feel the same, so actually look at the key. Please note, a good hotel does not have doors that

An LED on keychain helps you open hotel door at night.

lock by pulling shut; it has deadbolt locks. Unfortunately, roughly 50 percent of hotels are not up to speed.

6. Check the key to make sure it works when you are checking in, and of course make sure they give you the key. Do not allow the bellman to help you, when possible. There is no reason to educate him or her on how you manage your luggage.

7. Know who has the keys and how to call when checking in after regular business hours.

8. Never trust a hotel that hangs the room keys up behind the reception desk. Do not give the keys to them when you leave the hotel. Instead, try to put your own hasp on the door. ... Do anything to keep staff of this type of hotel from entering your room. They just do not care about having a secure hotel.

## Advisable Rules for Key Management

9. Our job at check-in is to get the key to our hotel room; the other information is the job of the hotel staff.

10. Always remove the huge hotel key tags (small ones also) and place the key onto your own key ring. You need to carry keys in a normal way for you and not the way the hotel wants. Remember, this is your home, so treat it as home.

11. When there are two people in a room, then get two keys, or don't check in. You will discover this to be a problem in most hotels.

12. Place your keys in the exact same location when you enter a hotel room, and never deviate.

13. Self-locking doors for hotel rooms are to be avoided. They are truly not safe, and you can easily lock yourself out.

14. Check your hotel key on adjoining doors. This is especially needed in primitive rooms with padlocks when you have not yet learned to use your own lock.

15. If you are living in a hotel for a month, then make extra key copies, the same as you would do at home.

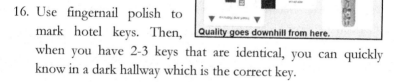

16. Use fingernail polish to mark hotel keys. Then, when you have 2-3 keys that are identical, you can quickly know in a dark hallway which is the correct key.

17. Do not carry your home keys with you outside your room. These keys should be in your money belt, neck pouch, secret pockets of travel pants, or remain in the hotel room.

18. When checking out, hand the keys directly to the hotel management and never the cleaning staff, maintenance man, etc.

19. Avoid skeleton keys. This is a sign the hotel is antiquated, in the dark ages of hotel management.

**Go online to add more rules or corrections to this topic; we will credit you in future additions. TheRulesofTravel.com/13**

# 14. Insurance

Insurance is pooling funds from a group of people to pay for one person's problem. We buy insurance to stop worrying where the money will come for specific problems. Insurance functions because people who do not use the insurance-pooled funds pay for those who do use the insurance.

U.S. employers and insurance companies do not benefit if you travel abroad. Because coverage for problems outside the USA is inadequate, your costs for problems escalate. Paying for problems overseas is 2-10 times more than if you stayed home.

For short-term trips abroad, most travelers have few problems. However, long-term travelers or other people living abroad need to stop relying on

Simple travel rule: Self-insurance (aka cash) is your best insurance abroad.

their home country's insurance and try buying insurance at their destination.

For example, if you moved from New York City to Tucson, Arizona, eventually you would change insurance agents. It is not practical to have your insurance company far from your home. The same is true for international travel. It is better to see if you can buy insurance in your destination country.

Internationally, medical services, doctors, laboratories, and medicines are available at locally affordable prices. The average person in more than 200 "less-developed" countries earns around 5-20 USD per day. Do the math! Medical care is quite affordable for American and European travelers in most of these countries, even without insurance.

## Non-Negotiable Travel Rules for Insurance

1. People without insurance can travel more easily than those with insurance. These people already do not have insurance; therefore, the financial risk is reduced in 200 of the normal countries. (The cost of doctors is often one dollar, and medicines cost about the same as a U.S. copay.)

2. Having the money to buy a plane ticket to the USA is travel insurance. 85-99 percent of medical problems can be delayed for a couple of days, and you can fly home, get American medical care, and pretend you never left.

3. You can return to the USA when you are very old and go on Medicaid. The less money you have, the more likely you are to be covered.

4. People who use insurance are likely to need insurance. If you are always using insurance, then international travel will be complicated.

5. Research how to buy local insurance at your destination, not from the USA.

6. You will never know if your insurance actually covers you until they pay.

7. Learn if your insurance pays to fly you home quickly.

If the U.S. government has a "do not visit" travel advisory, travel insurance is null and void.

8. Buy plane ticket insurance if you are worried. It is not really that expensive and worth it to relieve your anxiety. But if you're not worried, then do not buy it.

9. Travel insurance often does not pay for services in countries with a "do not visit" warning from the U.S. government.

10. Health insurance in the 200 more poor countries is one-fifth the cost of the 50 more expensive countries.

## Advisable Travel Rules for Insurance

11. You can live without insurance. That is obvious.

12. The goal of insurance companies is to scare you into buying their policies.

**Go online to add more rules or corrections to this topic; we will credit you in future additions. TheRulesofTravel.com/14**

# 15. Laptop Computers

Information in one's personal computer is worth a million dollars to us; it is irreplaceable. Dropping a laptop computer in the airport will destroy most computers; a baby is more durable than a computer. One sip of beer can destroy a laptop computer in seconds, yet even a novice photographer can easily photograph many users in public with beer or coffee next to a laptop computer.

Computer users assume we are perfect, that somehow we are exempt from making human errors. Well, there is one thing certain in life: Computers and humans are not perfect.

## Non-Negotiable Travel Rules for Laptop Computers

1. The computer is cheap; the information is expensive.

2. Drinks are not allowed to fly in the airspace above a computer.

3. Working on a computer in public makes you a target of computer theft.

4. Do not do Windows updates.

5. Buy computer bags that do not look like computer bags.

6. Never walk over the cord of a laptop computer.

7. A slow computer means you need to run a disk cleanup to remove temporary files.

8. Carry a computer long enough, and you will drop it.

9. Do not allow others to drop your computer. (Do not allow them to carry it ever – never, under any circumstance.)

10. Laptops fall from tables and chairs faster than the floor.

11. Do not carry the laptop with one hand.

12. Carry your laptop in front of you when there is danger around.

13. Vibration and bouncing in the back of a bus, truck, or shuttle are dangerous to laptops.

Keeping my laptop above the flood-line

14. Check the screws of your computer to make sure they are tight.

15. Playing music on a computer in public makes the computer a target of theft.

16. People that carry bags like to throw or drop the bags.

17. Keep your foot in the strap of a computer laptop bag when standing, sitting, talking, etc. in public in all countries on the planet.

18. A laptop computer is more likely to be stolen in rich countries. Generally, the poor countries have little use for a computer,

and they are not that easy to sell. However, music devices and cell phones are valuable everywhere.

19. Beer or soft drinks and computers do not mix.

20. Always know how to replace your computer from any country.

21. It is easy to travel to a country that does not sell Apple products.

Shoe repairman in Lima, Peru, is modifying my backpack to securely, discretely hold my laptop.

22. Computer bags that look like computer bags make you the target of computer thieves.

23. A computer cannot fall from the floor.

24. Do not often plug and unplug the power cord from the laptop: The female docking for the male connector will break inside the computer.

25. Keep the computer higher than your drinks.

26. In each country, calculate the time to replace your laptop computer in days. This is how long your boss will believe you are stupid when you lose or break your computer.

## Advisable Travel Rules for Laptop Computers

27. The ability to type information into a computer with all 10 fingers is a skill that all children need in this world.

28. The cloud will force you to buy software.

29. It is a 95 percent chance that an overheating computer needs internal dust cleaned out.

**Go online to add more rules or corrections to this topic; we will credit you in future additions. TheRulesofTravel.com/15**

# 16. Laundry

Laundry ... Laundry is an enigmatic problem for the world traveler.

How people manage their laundry is a "tell" about what kind of traveler they are, whether they have the ability to wander the entire planet or need to stick to 2-3 overly developed countries.

A. **Travelers who need their mothers with them** – These people travel with their friend, spouse, girlfriend, or boyfriend and let this person figure out how to get things done for them. These two people can travel the world together because one person is capable of world travel. These people generally set up in expat colonies or other specific locations to keep the helpless member of the two from abusing the other, more capable person.

B. **Travelers who can take care of themselves** – These travelers find economical ways of having their laundry done. They can be independent world travelers, visit over 50 countries outside of Europe, and freely wander the planet.

C. **Travelers who refuse to hand-wash their clothing** – These people should travel only to resorts or on tours, and for vacations less than 10 days long.

I carry a bucket with me. It was a large vegetable oil container, and I cut the top off and put a rope on it to use as a handle. I have used this every day of my life for the last 8-10 years. There are so many things I use it for as a traveler, I would never leave home without it. And I would never buy a backpack that was not large enough to put this tub inside.

## Non-Negotiable Travel Rules for Getting Your Laundry Done

1.  Finding a place to do laundry economically starts on the first day you arrive at a destination, and you have only 5-10 days before you need to find a laundry for around 5 USD for all your clothes.

    For having my laundry done by a machine or hand-washed by others, I budget 15-20 USD per month. If the cost will be higher than that or I will overrun my budget, I hand-wash my laundry myself. I refuse to pay 10 USD a load, for example, which comes out to 80 USD per month and 960 USD per year – the price of flying to anywhere on the planet one-way. This would require I work eight hours per day for laundry – not part of a savvy, world-traveler lifestyle.

    As you can see, most people cannot afford to travel; they can only afford to work.

2.  Weigh your clothes every chance you get. This will keep you from paying too much and being cheated when the scales weigh cloths at double or triple their real weight. Generally, do not worry much about the weight, but do try to ensure you spending within your laundry budget for a load. For me, that it is 3-5 USD. Generally, I am the only tourist or traveler in my group of friends that gets this good deal. The others just use

the most convenient laundry facility. I live a life of luxury and never wear dirty clothes. I can buy bright white and colorful clothing, never darks, because I know how to find budget pricing for laundry.

3. If you find a girlfriend in one of the 200 underdeveloped countries, you must allow her to do the laundry if she wants. To refuse her is to say she is not capable of being a good wife, and this is an insult.

4. If your friend needs help with laundry – a mother, wife, mate, or someone to clean his or her clothing – leave this person because you are becoming that person's cleaning person. Know your position in the relationship and do not become this person's servant, unless this is really what you choose with open eyes. 80-90 percent of husband/wife, girlfriend/boyfriend relationships end when the couple go on a long-term, around-the-world trip. If you want to stay married, do not travel the planet together.

5. The price of laundry should never be more than one-half–a-day's pay for a person in that country. 200 countries on the planet have an average pay of 3-10 USD per day. Many times, I am in locations where the tourist industry wants tourist-trap prices. Instead, I hire a local person to work half a day, clean my room, wash my cloths, and do chores because the tourist laundries are unjustly priced.

6. Know how many pieces of clothing you gave to the laundry. Unfortunately, they often try to mix your clothes in with other

peoples and are not organized; you need to know which pieces you gave them. When you find a laundry that does the job right, tell everyone so that this laundry thrives.

7. Never, ever, under any conditions give your laundry to be washed on the day before you fly out to go to your next destination. You need two days minimum to have your laundry done. Getting your laundry done the day before you fly out is a classic newbie traveler mistake.

8. Ask how the laundry is dried, and if they say dryer, go and physically inspect the dryer because 50-80 percent of laundries lie. Require they use the dryer; do not allow them to hang them on the line to save money. It is absolutely amazing how few laundries can be trusted on methods and the accuracy of their scales.

9. A five-star hotel or a resort needs to have a laundry facility where you drop off in the morning and the clothes are returned at night. If you are in a hotel with a 50 USD per day or higher rate and the hotel does not have that capacity, you are paying too much. Business travelers need to work, not deal with laundry, and the hotel should make laundry a non-issue for them.

10. Never over-pay a person to do your laundry. You are not doing this person a favor; you only enable them to believe you are stupid. If they get away with it, they will be stupid with other travelers again and again. It is a highly irresponsible traveler who inflates the prices in a country.

## Advisable Travel Rules for Getting Your Laundry Done

11. The clothing will be washed in local water. If you are inside a large city, this is a problem; often the water is so polluted that you will have trouble ever having clothes smell good. The solution is to make sure they have a heated dryer system; this kills smells and other fungus-type things that live in cold water and make it smell. It is not a perfect system, and staying out of large cities is always the best choice for a leisurely lifestyle.

12. Hang clothing on the line wrong-side out; they will dry faster.

13. Clothes under a fan will dry at about the same speed as clothes on a clothes line outside the room. Generally, the line is good, but in Central and South America, the locals will steal your clothing, so take care.

14. While clothing dries on a clothes line, rotate the pieces vertically so the clothes will dry faster.

15. Change your clothing often so that you do not badly soil your clothing, because this is very difficult to clean by hand.

16. Wash your clothing one time per month at a laundry with a dryer to get them very clean. And the dryer will shrink the collars of t-shirts, and stretched underwear will shrink back into shape.

17. Super-heat water and place your clothing into it one time per month. This will kill fungi and other skin-causing problems. 90 percent of the laundries on the planet never use hot water. Hot

water is the essential disinfectant for the body, 10 times better than using chemicals.

18. 50-100 country travelers need to carry a clothesline in their luggage.

19. Your body is easy to clean. Do not dirty your clothing in the room: Do not walk around on dirty floors in stocking feet and take your clothes off when inside a hotel room. It is easy to soil clothing, but difficult to hand wash.

20. Fans dry will dry clothes, but moving air with no sun takes five times longer.

21. When interviewing retire-abroad locations, ask the people trying to help you for specific explanations on the cost of laundry. A savvy person is going to be able to explain the cost, where to do your laundry, and pros and cons of laundry management. A person who is not capable of doing laundry is not a good consultant for travel or retirement because he or she does not understand the basic needs of human beings, one of which is laundry.

**Go online to add more rules or corrections to this topic; we will credit you in future additions. TheRulesofTravel.com/16**

# 17. Lovers Abroad

In an honest and intimate moment, even the most jaded human admits he or she wants to love and be loved.

It pains me to listen to couples, mothers, fathers, friends and family, brothers and sisters, Christians, Buddhists, Muslims, and every other combination of frail humanity neglect, belittle, and often mock love, as if people are stupid to not already be married with children, living happily ever after in the suburbs.

### Lovers Abroad?
**There comes a time when sensible people accept that love can be found in other places than home.**

One minute humans are macho, as if talking about love is taboo, and then they spend 5-10 hours per day searching for friendship and making friends, the little brother of love.

These rules on lovers abroad focus on how to stay out of the cliché, stereotypical lover dilemmas of fellow travelers. This is with the hope that we can all find love without setting ourselves up for heartbreak.

Friends and family often encourage you to beat a dead horse, stay in the same location, and never find a mate, friend, or someone else to love you and for you to love. After a few years of trying, there comes a time for change – and the sooner the better.

There is a country, a place, a location on the planet where another person dreams of finding a person just like you. Do not allow yourself or your friends to denigrate your hopes, as if all love is about money. Even in the USA, people marry for a bundle of reasons, such as having a good job, social status, or education. Yes, we must make ourselves lovable by having a lot to bring to the relationship.

Note: I hope and dream that everyone breaks all these rules below, yet still finds love in all the wrong places, but with all the right people. Love really seems to be an endless belief in serendipitous good fortune.

## Non-Negotiable Travel Rules for Lovers Abroad

1.  Do not talk with people who mock you about whom you love, how you love, or where you love.

2.  We can travel to countries where lovers are easy to find.

3.  The first one to marry is the one who says they will never marry.

4.  Do not send money by Western Union.

5.  Take a photo of your lover's identification card.

6.  Meet your lover's family on the second date.

7. Find lovers with jobs.

8. Do not buy a house for his or her family.

9. Do not date the tour guide.

10. The story starts with your lover saying, "I need money for …"

Love is everywhere!

11. Say you love them, and pay to prove it.

12. Beware of emotional vampires, people who need to feel stronger, more powerful in a relationship.

13. Love is staying, not leaving.

14. We can fall in love with a prostitute.

15. Know what the lover brings to the relationship.

16. Loving a person is not doing them a favor.

17. Love is after you become bored with sex.

18. Admit when you are not searching for love.

19. Great sex is not love.

20. Do not date men who come up to you in tourist spots.

21. Learn the culture of men who service women so you can avoid them … or find them.

22. Learn the culture of prostitutes, so you can avoid them … or find them.

23. Location is everything. A city with tons of prostitutes makes it impossible to find lovers. Where you go determines what you'll find.

24. Prostitutes don't make good girlfriends.

25. Know the lingo of prostitutes if you want to avoid them.

**Go online to add more rules or corrections to this topic; we will credit you in future additions. TheRulesofTravel.com/17**

# 18. Medicine

In more than 200 countries on the planet, medicines commonly prescribed in the USA are sold over the counter without a prescription. We only need to walk into the pharmacy, request the medicine we desire, and they will sell it to us, about the same as buying aspirin inside the USA.

There are approximately 50 over-developed countries on the planet where we will have major problems buying medicines.

**Well-stocked pharmacies are found worldwide – Don't panic!**

Strangely, traveling in the 200 poorer countries is often medically safer because we can afford the medicines and buy them easily. The risk is that we can misuse or abuse the medicines.

These rules of medicine prepare you to communicate with pharmacists and doctors abroad. In the event you are robbed or becoming incapacitated, other people will be able to assist you quickly.

Please do not worry: There are medicines available in almost any country on the planet; the pharmaceutical companies sell everywhere. And they lower or increase the prices so that locals can buy the drugs. Escaping the financial chokehold of the U.S. medical community will be a freedom you will love.

After 15 years of living outside the USA, if I had a major medical problem inside the USA, I would fly to foreign countries for treatment. What costs me 50 USD inside the USA only costs 5 USD in the 200 normal countries — same medicines, just adjusted down to the cheaper countries' ability to pay. It feels good to buy fairly priced medicines.

## Non-Negotiable Travel Rules for Medicines

1.  Assume when you travel abroad that you will become confused, disoriented, and incapable of thinking for yourself. You need to assist people around you to know your medical needs, whether the ailments or the medicines. They need this information when you are not capable of explaining. There is gossip that people will just let you die. That is an oversimplification of a difficult situation. The world wants to know how you are going to pay for the hospital and doctor. You need to make them aware; this is your responsibility, not theirs.

    Fortunately, 99 percent of travel health problems you can be solved by walking into a pharmacy, explaining the problem, and receiving the medicine with little or no fuss and no prescription needed.

2.  Take photos of all your medicines and store the photos in email folder so you can access them from anywhere on the

planet. Pharmacist can read the labels and figure out what medicines you need.

3. Carry 10 day's more medicine than the number of days of your trip. If, for example, you are going on 10-day cruise, carry 20 days of the prescribed medicines you need. Then, if you are injured and need to stay in a hospital for five days, there would be no disruption in your meds.

4. Buy malaria medicine in countries with malaria and carry it home with you. In the event you suddenly feel like a wet rag and you cannot move, take the medicine. U.S. doctors are not prepared to deal with malaria.

5. Do not assume you are talking with a licensed, educated pharmacist abroad; often it is just a normal person off the street. The solution is to go to 3-4 pharmacies, and keep asking questions until you feel safe

6. Know that health insurance generally does not pay for medicines in countries where there is a consular warning to not visit. (See the fine print in your policy.)

7. If you are taking highly controlled medicines, such as opiates, Codeine or Valium, makes sure you have copies of prescriptions and the telephone numbers of the doctors that prescribed them. Even though you may be able to buy these medicines across the counter, it does not grant you the right to become a drug addict. The wrong perception by the

pharmacist could land you in a jail overseas. Do not play games; be transparent and honest.

8. Do not carry every possible medicine; they sell most medicines in all countries for 5-10 times less money.

## Advisable Travel Rules for Medicines

9. Search on Wikipedia.org for your medicines and maladies, and click on the left hand side for your destination's language when possible. This will lead you to a page that will translate the information. Download these as PDF files and store them inside a folder in your email account. Then you have access to them anywhere on the planet.

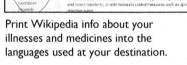

10. Print out the medicine' photos and the translated Wikipedia.org pages, and carry them with you in the country you are visiting.

Print Wikipedia info about your illnesses and medicines into the languages used at your destination.

11. Email these PDFs and photos to 2-3 friends. Ask them to leave them in their email inbox and not delete them.

12. Place notes in the emergency pages of your passport explaining who has access to this information.

13. Make 1-4 cards in the language of your destination country explaining who to contact in an emergency. Place these in many locations: backpacks, day bags, purses, wallets, etc.

14. Complete the linked CDC travel information and obey instructions. http://www.bt.cdc.gov/disasters/pdf/kiwy.pdf

15. Avoid tourist trap pharmacies. Many expat and tourist areas have pharmacies that prey on your naive understanding of the countries. These often do not even have educated staff, just a regular person to man the store, and they can be dangerous. It

is best to travel far as possible away from the tourist bubble to where normal people live to find the better pharmacies.

16.     Do not allow or trust local friends from the country to translate and help you to buy medicines. You need a person from your same country to help you, one who speaks both your language and the local language. You do not want your medical needs lost in translation.

17. People that would die without certain medicines should not travel alone; they need to be with friends or on a tour. This will ensure they will have someone to take care of them properly.

18. Do not take anti-malaria medicines for more than 14 days. These medicines are not considered safe by normal long-term travelers; we refuse to take them.

19. Doctors are often free in other countries, and you pay for the medicines.

20. Carry the packaging of medicines with you so that they are easy to read by the pharmacist.

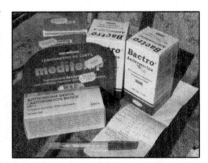

Bring medicine packaging with you.

21. Malaria is curable and is called "puludisme" in French, but it is normally called malaria in most countries. You do not die quickly from malaria.

22. Do your research, and do not listen to idle comments from friends. 90 percent of their advice is of zero value and is often dangerously wrong. Wikipedia is the best place to do your research. Medical sites are often sales sites and will mislead you for profit.

**Go online to add more rules or corrections to this topic; we will credit you in future additions. TheRulesofTravel.com/18**

# 19. Money in Cash

The banks, credit unions, airlines – anybody and everybody – want us to stop using cash money. And many people freely admit, "I am no good at math." Cash makes them nervous.

Cash is simple: When you spend money, the cash leaves your pocket, and what remains is how much money you have left to spend.

These cash money rules make the math simple, empowering travelers to stop ranting:

– "The hotel cheated us."

– "The airline cheated us."

– "The credit card company cheated us."

Dinar's Saddam Hussein
EINSTEIN
100 Dollars
Heavy Money

In this blog article, we are not explaining the reasons, the "whys" for cash money rules. The whys can be confusing, but experienced travelers have learned them the hard way: We lost money, were cheated, robbed, scammed ... and on and on.

Avoid our mistakes! Obeying the rules is easy and will stop you from being cheated, help you budget, and keep your travel simple.

## Non-Negotiable Travel Rules for Money in Cash

1.  People with correct change in their pockets are clever.

2.  Opening a wallet full of cash or credit cards in front of people makes you a target of crime.

3.  Cash stops unexpected travel costs.

4.  A 10 USD bill in 200 countries is a day's pay.

5.  Carry only the cash you wish to spend today.

6.  Never carry a wallet in your back pocket.

7.  Money changers always cost money to use.

8.  Earning more than 1.25 USD per day means the person is not poor.

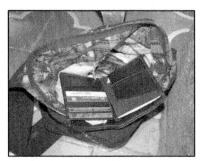

Pulling out a wallet full of cash and credit cards in public invites theft.

9.  Leave your money belt or neck pouch in your hotel room.

10. Every chance you get, change large bills into smaller ones.

11. Carry new 100 USD bills when you leave the USA.

12. Keep enough cash in your room to pay 5-7 days of your hotel bill.

## Advisable Travel Rules for Money in Cash

13. Do not carry a wallet.

14. Carry U.S. dollars, not Euros. You can carry both, but never carry only Euros.

15. Do not make change for people using your cash.

16. Have small change with you at all times.

17. Do not give large bills to people who earn 10 USD per day.

18. Do not hand cash to people or count money in public. Yet you need to pay the tour operator, the hotel, or the store in public and have witnesses.


**Go online to add more rules or corrections to this topic; we will credit you in future additions. TheRulesofTravel.com/19**

# 20. Passports

Having a passport is proof of citizenship abroad. Without it, we are an illegal alien and can be taken to jail or deported.

It is obvious that Americans, Canadians, Europeans, Australians, New Zealanders, Japanese, and South Koreans have special status as travelers. The people from the 50 rich countries on the planet

are given graces and favors the other 200 are not allowed. What we 50 rich-countries people can do is radically different than what the 200-plus poor-countries people are allowed.

A first world passport opens doors ... but it's no guarantee of favorable treatment.

But to expect the letter of the law and justice to prevail is naïve. Plan for the worst and hope for the best ... and have plenty of time available for problems.

Arriving late at the airport with your new Thai wife who is traveling on a U.S. passport is a recipe for problems. You do not deserve passport problems in a perfect world, but you deserve what you get in an imperfect world.

## Non-Negotiable Travel Rules for Passports

1. Hassle-free travel is easy by traveling only in the USA with your American passport and never internationally.

2. Contempt on our face and passports do not make good travel companions.

3. The passport is the only thing you cannot forget to pack.

4. Be the obvious holder of the passport and able to defend its culture.

   It is like a tragic comedy when U.S. citizens are standing in the U.S. customs lines, ready to enter the USA after visiting abroad. There are many U.S. citizens who do not speak English, who appear as citizens of the country of my plane departure. For example, if I am flying from Peru to the USA, the U.S.-only line at customs is full of people that obviously appear Peruvian. They do not obviously appear American, and they often do not speak English, and they do not understand the customs and culture of America.

   They are not going to have problems returning to the USA, but traveling to other countries can be an extreme hassle if you are not an obvious, stereotypical person from the country of passport.

   When an American goes abroad and finds a wife or husband – and subsequently receives a passport for the new spouse – he or she should plan on having problems traveling with the new spouse. Having a passport alone is not proof of American citizenship. Yes, it is with enough time, but you can be delayed for hours or days without supporting evidence, such as driver's licenses or voter registration cards. It is based on a preponderance of evidence, and racial profiling is standard in the world, not rare.

5. Leave your passport in your hotel room. (Or know why you are breaking this rule!!!)

6. Scan your passport and email it to yourself. Store the digital copy in a free email account, such as Yahoo.com or Gmail.com. Company accounts or paid accounts, such as Frontier, Comcast, Verizon, and AOL.com, will cause you problems traveling abroad. They are signs the traveler is not really ready to travel.

7. NEVER, ever say, "I am American; you cannot do that to me." Saying this will make – nay, require – the country's law enforcement to "prove" to you that you do not have rights. They will take your passport and make you stand around for hours or days learning this hard truth.

8. Do not store your passport in a safe at the hotel reception desk.

9. U.S. passports do not grant you American rights in other countries.

10. Whoever has your passport can make you buy it back.

11. You need to speak the language of your passport country.

12. New citizens of the USA need to carry their passports always.

13. Passports are easy to replace when lost or stolen. But they require you make a trip to an American embassy in the destination country.

14. Visa stamps make the passport expensive to replace.

15. Do not show your passport to people.

16. You can keep expired passports as souvenirs.

Visa stamps make the passport expensive to replace.

17. Do not carry your passport everywhere you go.

18. Passports get moldy in airtight plastic bags.

19. All papers given to you at a border stay with your passport. I remember getting some weird piece of paper as I entered the Philippines. As I exited, immigration wanted this paper back. The man next to me needed to pay the country 20 USD because he could not find it. Governments are clever; they want extra fees and are willing to give you papers to lose.

20. Do not allow immigration staff to write information on your passport. Do not allow them to write "carrying a computer" or "with wife" or other information. When you leave the country, this information becomes a red flag, a problem.

21. Store your passport in the same location in every hotel.

22. Do not hide your passport in places that are not packed. Putting your passport under the mattress is going to help you to forget the passport. Hiding it in the pants pocket of a pair of pants folded neatly and stacked in the closet is a guarantee it is not going to travel to the airport with you.

23. Carry a copy of your passport, as well as a copy of the visa stamp page. This is especially wise when you're nervous inside a country.

24. Roadblocks want to see the visa stamp on your passport. Be ready and open to the page, and then they know you are savvy.

25. People with fat passports need to know which page the visa stamp is on, especially when you have 2-10 from the country you are departing.

26. Fill out the "in case of emergency" page.

27. Do not hand your passport to the police.

28. A U.S. passport is replaceable if lost or stolen.

29. U.S. embassies abroad can add extra pages.

30. Do not allow another person to pretend to be with you and your passport. Many smugglers and nefarious characters want to befriend you at border crossings in the hope the officials believe they are traveling with you.

## Advisable Travel Rules for Passports

31. Travel with photos and a birth certificate to apply for a new passport if needed.

32. If you speak the local language and look the same color or race as the country of destination, then carry your passport with you as you walk around outside the hotel room.

33. Handing your passport to immigration and saying "What's up?" is American culture.

**Go online to add more rules or corrections to this topic; we will credit you in future additions. TheRulesofTravel.com/20**

# 21. Plane In-Flight Comfort

An airplane flight is similar to being strapped into a seat and then thrown into solitary confinement. If planes were not the fastest way of travel, they would be avoided at all cost. Sitting in a small plane seat with nothing to see is by far the most boring and uncomfortable way of travel. Only the camel, donkey, and vans as alternatives to buses are worst.

Planes are cramped. Good neighbors are key to a good flight.

We seem to ignore the question, what did you see on the flight? In the past, airlines provided food, free drinks, newspapers, magazines, and movies for free. However, we are now responsible for making our in-flight trip comfortable.

Your main goals for the in-flight plane trip are having a comfortable seat by comfortable people and finding ways to relieve boredom while in solitary confinement.

Traveling the world is for people who like people. If you do not want to talk to anybody and everybody, then you truly need to stay home because world travel requires you to be social. And boarding a plane that is small, tight, and packed with seats just barely wider than the hips of an average person, coupled with randomly being seated next to strangers with no right to move, is dreadful travel.

These travel in-flight rules will help you adapt and optimize your flight.

## Non-Negotiable Rules for In-Flight Comfort

1.  Be the last person to board the plane. Do not volunteer to enter the cramped and claustrophobic quarters of an airplane until required.

    My friend Walt explains lines of people: "They learned to stand in line in kindergarten, and 50 years later than are still fighting to be first in line."

    Generally, there are 1-3 savvy travelers waiting to be last. They want to avoid the boarding line. Adapting to airplane flights is adapting; it is survival of the fittest, and there is no reason to enter a small compartment full of people until you are forced. We need to relax and sit back; the plane is not going to leave without you. Be the last to board; you walk in fast, with no need to wait, and the one or two stewardesses are available to help because they are finished with the other passengers.

2.  Be the last person to board the plane to choose the best seat. We do not allow an airline to make the rules; we make the rules. We choose the location, people, and benefits; it is our choice, and airlines really do try to please. Planes generally have 5-15 percent of the seats empty. This is a great benefit for the

savvy air traveler. I do not want first-class seating; I want 3-4 seats together where I can lie down and sleep through the whole flight, if possible. The plane stewardess does to not like you taking a seat and then moving from your assigned seat. However, if you are last, you can just choose any open seat or multiple seats. If you look around, maybe there are 3-4 seats open in a series. This is a good bed on a long-haul flight. If not, then you start to look for a good cellmate, someone who is friendly, small, and happy. We can afford to have great manners for one hour, but spending 8-13 hours next the wrong people is never a benefit.

3. Ask the stewardess to help you move seats away from passengers who are not acceptable, noisy, unfriendly, obese, smelly, ill-mannered, or disgusting. It is amazing: The stewardess has great empathy for this, and he or she will go to great lengths to make you happy.

4. Do not allow the stewardess to put your carry-on bag into a compartment behind you, only in front. And if there is a problem, get up when the plane takes off and move it; do not just agree to have problems. The secret to comfort is expecting comfort as a way of life.

5. Never give up a great seat just to be accommodating.

6. Eat the meal you want. Do not tolerate eating fish when you wanted beef. The problem is that airlines have learned passengers allow themselves to be victimized.

7. Carry a light blanket, sheet, or even a big towel onto a plane. You never know if there are going to be blankets on the plane. If the stewardess offers you one, take it; better to not need it than to need it later.

Carry a blanket on board.

8. Carry a headset so that you can hear the film. It is strange, but many airlines show videos with no way to hear the words. Plus, you need to have ear buds to watch a film on your computer. You can share them; one set can be shared by two people.

## Advisable Rules for In-Flight Comfort

9. Give the stewardess a big smile and greeting, and be fun. If you talk, you will enjoy the trip. And you can challenge the stewardess to feed you better than other passengers. I often board the plane and say, "Hello. Boy, I am hungry today. Are you going to feed me?"

10. Spot the complainers while sitting and waiting for the gate to open so that you know whom to avoid.

11. Lower the aisle seat handle or ask the stewardess to put down the handle so this seat is wider. It will be easier to enter and leave the seat.

12. Ask people to trade seats so that you can find a friend.

13. Do not sit down next to really large or obese people. Go back and talk with the stewardess and say, "I need another seat."

14. Look for seat belt extenders in empty seats, and if you see one, avoid the seat next to this person.

15. Travel with a friend to have a conversation.

16. Ask the people to stop snoring, playing music, talking loudly, or being annoying, and if you have a problem, request help from stewardess.

17. Elbow the person next to you or put your bag into his or her lap. Make the seat hogs grant you your full seat rights.

18. Really long-legged people can request the exit seat. It is wider, but often these seats do not recline.

19. Take Valium, Librium, downers, or get drunk, and wake up when you arrive. Please note that this is very dangerous on trains, vans, or buses, but passengers on planes are normally a better quality of human.

20. Have a bag that you can store under the seat. This allows you to open the bag, retrieve magazines, books, a computer, and other items without a problem.

21. Carry a DVD, computer, iPad, or other device that plays films.

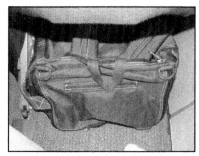

Have a bag that fits under seat for quick access to things you want during the flight, e.g., books, medicine.

22. Wear long pants, especially on long-haul flights. Airplane flights can be cold; you do not want to freeze for 10 hours.

23. Close the window to stop the sun entering the cabin, and even ask the people on the other side to close their window cover.

24. Use the restroom or toilet before you enter the plane – always a better option than the plane toilet.

25. Turn off the fan or redirect it. Do not be shy. Stand up and shut them off around you, or ask for assistance if you need it. Or do the same to turn them on, if that is what you prefer.

26. Check if the headrest is the wrap around your head type.

**Go online to add more rules or corrections to this topic; we will credit you in future additions. TheRulesofTravel.com/21**

# 22. Plane Tickets

Buying a plane ticket is like politics: The more we learn, the more we worry, so finally we make the decision to stop thinking and to buy peace of mind.

When someone says, you could have gotten a cheaper ticket, just say, "I know." Defending your plane ticket purchase price is like supporting the president of the United States: Everyone is an expert and wants to explain why you are not.

Knowing who paid the real money for the plane ticket is wise. I ate dinner one time with the "Charger" of the American embassy in

Togo, West Africa, and the wife of one of the many dinner guests said, "If you need to buy your own ticket, Air Moroc is much cheaper than Air France, like the embassy buys."

I thought to myself: "All these people in this room, except for me, work for the embassy. They have lost the plot because they do not buy their own tickets and willfully allow the government to pay too much. My tax dollars at work!"

Follow the money trail to learn who purchased plane tickets. If the company, charity, school, or tour company purchased the plane tickets, or there were inducements, for example, frequent flyer miles earned, then beware of the advice you hear. Really, it is just best to ignore these people. To learn how to buy cheap tickets, we must find people who paid cash, not credit, and painfully raised the money to pay for the plane fare.

In the end, plane tickets are the same as political decisions: We must choose the best from a list of bad choices, and seldom the plane ticket we wanted.

Buying plane tickets is a lesson in optimizing decisions. All the choices are dynamic: When one option is better, another option degrades. For example, you might get a better ticket price, but now you do not have a direct flight. Only you can make the optimal decision for you and your family.

Local hopper, Bolivia

## Non-Negotiable Travel Rules for Plane Tickets

1. Do not buy early and don't buy at last minute – Buy the best plane ticket.

2. The airlines will not allow you on the plane for an international flight without an onward ticket.

   **WARNING: Rule 2 disagrees with Rule 3!**

103

3. Buy only the plane tickets you plan to use.

   Many people buy roundtrip plane tickets because we are told we must or told that we cannot get on the plane without one. If you have the will, there is generally a way to avoid paying for extra plane tickets you neither need nor want. Please understand, you must arrange the onward or roundtrip plane ticket in advance, but there are many ways to avoid paying. A good travel agent can give you the ticket and a refund when you return. And savvy travelers know other tricks as well.

4. Do not burn bridges; do not click your email's spam button for travel site emails. For example, if you click the spam button on Kayak, Travelocity, or some travel company,

A good travel agent can still help you find the best deals.

   person, or organization that gives you advice, those websites will know and never write you again. And they cannot reply to your emails. Filter these emails or unsubscribe; clicking on the spam button is foolish. You might desperately need emails returned in the future, but when you click on the spam button, it is often an irreversible decision. You block business with this company forever.

5. Finding a better-priced plane ticket is not a reason to stop using a travel agent. Buying a plane ticket needs to be a group

effort. The more you help a travel agent, the better. On the other hand, if a travel agent treats you contemptuously for shopping around, it is time to change travel agents.

6. Business travelers who fly often are not experts.

7. Do not always use the same plane ticket website.

8. Do not buy roundtrip tickets unless you really want the return ticket.

9. Never tell the person next to you on the plane what you paid for your ticket.

10. Know someone who is better than you at buying tickets.

11. Companies pay 2-5 times more than needed for plane tickets.

12. When starting to buy on the Internet, click through to the end of the purchase process (without paying) for practice. This will help you understand the full price.

13. Take written notes on paper when buying tickets on the Internet. The websites of airlines are banking on the fact you cannot remember more than 1-2 screens back.

14. Charter plane tickets are generally the cheapest plane tickets.

15. Buy the final plane ticket on the airline's own website when possible. The service provided will be better if there are problems.

16. Join the plane ticket website before you buy the ticket.

17. Always have a way to pay baggage fees, even when you believe you do not owe baggage fees.

18. Check departure and arrival times of the trip.

19. Buying online is not the best way to find the cheapest plane tickets.

20. Know what a "low-cost carrier" means.

21. You need to know how to find a list of low-cost carriers if you want the cheapest plane tickets.

22. Buy flight insurance when flying from the USA to another country.

23. Find the best price on Internet, and then go buy from a travel agent.

24. Get your visa before your plane ticket. Yet often, you need the plane ticket to get the visa. This is a catch 22!

25. We will fly again on the airlines we say we will never use again.

26. The person with good plane ticket buying advice probably has a few photos of planes on his or her computer.

**Go online to add more rules or corrections to this topic; we will credit you in future additions. TheRulesofTravel.com/22**

# 23. Qualified Travel Resources

Travel information comes in three forms: facts, opinions, and buying options. The Internet provides all the facts of the world at our fingertips; the caveat is people then fail to double check with experts. Less than 10 percent of travel articles are written by people who actually traveled to the destination. Photos and information are copied, often-misrepresented opinions to earn commission from hotels and tours.

## Non-Negotiable Travel Rules for Qualified Travel Resources

1.  Good travel information resources are created by people who take credit and responsibility for their work.

2.  Start your travel research with facts. Generally, the best place to start is an encyclopedia, whether at your local library or Wikipedia.org online. Assume that all other resources are opinions. After you understand the facts, then read the opinions; you will then understand the quality of the opinions better.

3.  Ignore sources of information that always portray opinions as facts; this is not a trustworthy writing style.

4.  View all travel resources as advertisements whereby the writers could earn money by giving bad advice. Travel magazines are generally advertisements for large resorts and hotels. Public

relations firms, working for tourist bureaus, pay to have articles written and published in the magazines. Use magazine for ideas and inspiration, but buying is seldom wise.

5. Good travel information has editors who fact-check.

6. Do not follow anonymous advice. It is the enemy. Steer clear of this information. It is often misleading and normally expensive to follow. Sources like the New York Times and Guardian Newspaper have editors, staff, and writers with a reputation to defend.

7. Travel paper guidebooks are your best source of general travel destination information. Guidebooks give time-tested opinions on the best hotels in an area, maps, and transportation. Guidebooks save time and money. They are almost the only way to find the cheapest hotels in a city. Lonely Planet, Rough Guide, and Footprint are your globally astute brands.

8. Trendiness is maybe for restaurants, but risking your vacation on a trendy hotel, trendy tour, and trendy tweet is not wise; trendy is not wisdom.

9. Best advice comes from people who give their full name, address, and biography with a photo. These people are willing take responsibility for their opinions.

10. Videos are always better than photos; it is very easy to hide information using photos.

11. Information published on paper is better than Internet-based information.

12. Reviews of hotels are gamed by hotels. They pay people to write reviews. If you cannot stop reading them, then look at very absolute, specific comments, e.g., "the room smelled moldy."

13. The best price for plane tickets could be anywhere. Try everything possible, and avoid believing people who say they only use Kayak, Expedia, or their favorite travel agent. There is always a better-priced ticket to be purchased.

14. When at a travel destination, first ask advice from other foreigners before the locals. The foreigners empathize with your problems, while locals want to make money. For example, locals do not exchange money or sleep in a hotel. What would they know about these topics?

15. When talking with a human, ask him or her when he or she was last at the destination? This is an amazing thing! You will discover that people are willing to talk as if they know about a place they have never visited, and it is an eye opener.

## Primary Sources of Travel Information

A. Paper Guidebooks

B. Travel page of large newspapers

C. Travel books written by one author, with no products or tours sold

D. Free magazines at the travel destination

E. Wikipedia.org, Britannica, World Book Encyclopedias

Please avoid TripAdvisor, Yelp, Facebook, Twitter, or any trendy sources of information; they will confuse you. It will be like chasing your tail. Any source of information that is not obviously based on facts compiled by one person or business team is gossip. Reading gossip and opinions detracts from the time spent learning from experts.

**Go online to add more rules or corrections to this topic; we will credit you in future additions. TheRulesofTravel.com/23**

# 24. Restaurants

"Where are we going to eat?"

This question is often heard in the developed world, those richest

Obama Rice – Coincidence or sharp marketing?

50 countries, which have a surplus of choices for restaurants and cuisines. The best restaurants for Mexican or Indian food are seldom in the countries of origin. The 50 overdeveloped countries are spinning and evolving. The competition is fierce.

The leisure-style eating of the USA is in many ways a tourist attraction. Trying something new, that new restaurant that just opened, and then discussing the merits is the American way. But those customs backfire on ignorant American travelers.

Diarrhea, food poisoning, and paranoia spoil many vacations. And it is normal to hear travelers blaming a restaurant for becoming sick. Instead, take responsibility for your health and follow the rules.

## Non-Negotiable Travel Rules for Restaurant

1. Uncooked food causes food-borne illness.

2.  Dishes are washed in water that we are not supposed to drink.

3.  Know how to cure food poisoning.

4.  The bigger the menu, the more dangerous the food is to eat. There are menus that are books, but if you stop and look around, you will realize it is not possible to have that much fresh food ready to cook in their stockpiles of food. Simple menus are manageable, and the food turnover is fast.

5.  Saying which restaurant made you sick is an educated guess at best.

6.  Do not eat in restaurants that are always empty.

7.  Do not eat too much of one food. Most diarrhea is from eating too much of a food you love and that is not easy to buy at home, yet is everywhere in the new location. This type of diarrhea goes away when you stop eating the food and allow it to pass through your body.

8.  Combinations of food cause people to get sick.

9.  Going more than 100 miles from one's home causes diarrhea in many people. There are different strains of bacteria, and many people are sensitive and develop light cases of diarrhea. This is natural; don't blame the restaurant for everything.

## Advisable Travel Rules for Restaurants

10. Get to know the cook before you eat.

11. Don't eat in restaurants where they hide the cook or chef.

12. Using reviews for restaurants is dangerous. Reviews are gamed by the restaurants.

Don't eat at restaurants that hide the cook from you.

13. A good location to retire abroad normally has a couple of safe restaurants where the old-timer expats hang out and eat.

**Go online to add more rules or corrections to this topic; we will credit you in future additions. TheRulesofTravel.com/24**

# 25. Retirement Abroad

Retirement abroad is extremely safe when you follow the rules ... or one of the worst investments known to man if you don't. People

Popular retirement destination – Dominican Republic

scream at us, tell us daily, "the country is corrupt, the police want bribes, etc." And many people who retire abroad and still believe they can trust a foreign government take their life savings, their life's work, and gamble it away.

Retirement abroad is living in your favorite foreign country. But of people who retire abroad, roughly 95 percent die in their country of citizenship.

## Non-Negotiable Rules of Retirement Abroad

1.  Do not buy real estate abroad because you will lose money. Of course, you can buy real estate knowing that you are going to lose the money invested. The belief that one cannot lose money in real estate abroad is false when you can lose your whole investment easily.

2.  Do not use the fear of visa limitations as a reason not to live in a country. Immigration restrictions are almost irrelevant. Generally, there is a way to live in all countries. Think about

this: There are business ventures from the USA in all countries, and they grant a way for these people to live there. There are only 1-3 countries on the planet that are close to impossible for retirement abroad.

3. Do not tell the insurance companies you are living abroad. Health insurance, life insurance, and the U.S. government deserve as little information as possible. Organizations, governments, and companies will use this information against you, making it an excuse to deny you service or rights.

4. Decide where you are going to die, as well as the city, country, and people who are going to assist you when you become physically disabled. Retirement abroad does not mean you have to die abroad. Living abroad is a different decision than where to die. However, your exit strategy becomes essential when you move away from lifelong family, friends, hospitals, Medicare, and Medicaid.

5. Always have enough cash money to buy a plane ticket back to the USA or your home country. If you are running out of money, make the decision to fly home before you use all your money. You need a minimum of 2,000 USD in your bank account ready for problems that only money will solve.

6. Know the amount of time it takes to reverse a decision. Many people live abroad long after they want to leave, because they refuse to lose money when their dream house never sells, and they know if they leave it, the locals will move in and steal everything.

7.  Your U.S. dollars abroad will be nationalized and the money turned into local currency. When the country has a financial crisis, e.g., Argentina 1999-2002, you will lose your money's value. So keep some money in U.S. banks or cash.

8.  Find a person who will mail you ATM cards, credit cards, and important papers if you are incapable of flying home. Trusted people at home make it easier to live abroad. But be warned: Many a wife or husband, children, or friends have been granted power of attorney and taken all the money out of a person's accounts.

9.  Do not make an application for residency unless you are absolutely forced to, for example, if you need it to buy a business or you cannot marry without it. There are a few good reasons but many more many bad ones. When you declare residency, you are signing up to pay taxes, become part of their computer database, and become accountable to two countries.

10. You will never have enough money to move abroad, so you need to move abroad when you want and trust that everything has a solution.

## Advisable Rules for Retirement Abroad

11. Visit at least three prospective locations. Often people do not feel they have the money to do this or the time. In reality, this is one of the most life-changing decisions you can make. Spend the money and take the time. It is the best investment you can make.

12. Learn the language of the country where you wish to retire for reading leases, understanding prices, etc. Generally, people who do not speak the local language pay 50-100 percent more.

13. Do not register with a U.S. embassy or give the CIA, INS, or any U.S. government agency notice you are in your new live-abroad country. When your passport was swiped at immigration, that information became the knowledge of the USA and your host country. That is enough.

**Go online to add more rules or corrections to this topic; we will credit you in future additions. TheRulesofTravel.com/25**

# 26. Taking Photos

As world travelers, we want to take great photos and not annoy the locals at our travel destination. We want to be responsible travelers who are sensitive to our hosts, but we also want to take photos to remember our trip. This is a difficult balance to achieve; however, long-term travelers know that taking photos is not harming the planet or anyone in particular, really.

First we must decide our ethical point of view, choosing between two options:

A. It is OK to take photos in public areas without permission.

    -OR-

B. It is NOT OK to take photos in public areas; we need to always ask permission.

Street singer, Tobago

This is the essential problem we face taking photos: We must make a commitment to one or the other. Until we make this decision, we are forever confused, and this confusion makes being a photographer difficult.

Paparazzi defined: Paparazzi are photographers who take pictures by invading others' personal spaces and private areas, taking photos without consent to sell or use for profit.

## Non-negotiable Photo Rules

1.  There is no right to privacy in public places, e.g., beaches, tourist areas, outside of buildings, restaurants, etc. Take the photos without asking permission.

2.  There is a right to privacy in members-only-type areas, e.g., churches, synagogues, homes, etc. Do not take photos unless you have permission.

3.  People doing private things in public can be photographed. They are annoying the public. It is not their right to do private things in public and expect privacy; it is an inappropriate expectation.

4.  Never pay for taking photos, unless you will really need to because you will never see the subject again. Paying to take photos is closer to a bribe than a purchase. If you really want to purchase the right, then get a release and a receipt for your money. However, bribe payments can result in the person coming to you every day and begging for money.

5.  People posing are agreeing to have their photo taken. If they ask to have their photo taken, never feel as though you need to assist, alter or change photos for them later. They suspended their rights by posing.

## Advisable photo rules:

6. Do not ask for permission. Just give a big smile and assume that everyone loves their photo taken. When you ask, that grants power to the subject of your photo, and we do not want them to decide how you take photos. We want to rely only on our own skill and intuition to take our best photos.

7. The sun should be behind you as you take photos.

8. Include the feet; it will normally make for better photos.

9. Click slowly until the camera focuses; a quick snap can allow badly focused photos.

10. New batteries in your camera will let you take better photos.

11. Carry extra batteries with you.

12. Do not ask 1-3 people to say "cheese." This will cause the people to flinch or look like mummies. Try instead to make them laugh, and then take many photos.

13. If you are taking a photo of a person with a background of a tourist attraction, then take 10-20 photos. This will guarantee one good photo.

14. Learn how to take a time-delayed photo; it comes in handy.

**Go online to add more rules or corrections to this topic; we will credit you in future additions. TheRulesofTravel.com/26**

# 27. Taxis

One day, we will all become too old to drive a car, and taxis are a great alternative. But the average American or European will say,

Bicycle-powered taxis, Nepal

"They are too expensive to use."

As world travelers, we often take 2-10 taxi trips per day, costing on average 0.50-1.00 USD per trip.

I hope every person on the planet one day lives in a city with cheap taxis.

## Non-Negotiable Travel Rules for Taxis

1.  The best taxi driver is also the best tour guide.

2.  Taxi drivers are city maps in disguise.

3.  Taxis are safer than driving a rental car.

4.  Taxis will not drive you into dangerous neighborhoods.

5.  Taxi drivers do not have change for money for a reason.

6.  Use the same taxi drivers daily.

7. Stand on the same side of the road as the direction you are going.

8. Overpaying taxis inflates the cost for the locals.

9. Read the eyes of the taxi driver when asking questions. Taxi drivers lie with their mouths and tell the truth with their eyes.

10. Telephoning for a taxi costs more than flagging one down in the street.

11. Do not use a parked taxi when very hot; flag down one that is moving or fully air conditioned.

12. Good hotels advise you how to handle taxis.

13. Moving taxis are cheaper.

14. Choose the driver, not the taxi.

15. Give half the money to the taxi when it enters a gas station.

Taxi *motocicleta*, Cuba

16. Have the correct change.

17. Know the price before you enter a taxi.

18. If cheated, take a photo of the taxi plate.

19. Only pay a taxi with credit card in your home country.

20. Know what a collective taxi is.

21. Collective taxis are great for meeting locals.

22. If you walk out of the airport you will get a better price.

## Advisable Travel Rules for Taxis

23. Know the direction of your taxi trip.

24. Taxi stands cost more than moving taxis.

25. Do not walk across a highway to meet a taxi.

26. Don't ask the taxi driver the prices; ask a local.

27. When departing the plane on arrival, walk to the airport arrival area and flag down a taxi. The taxis dropping off people to depart by plane are not airport taxis and will give discounted standard city taxi fares.

Stop driving cars. Using taxis is true freedom from debt.

**Go online to add more rules or corrections to this topic; we will credit you in future additions. TheRulesofTravel.com/27**

# 28. Tour Guides

There are many kinds of travel tours, but normally, the best tour guide is one from your home country, working in partnership with people in the destination country.

Often, many tour companies share the same tourist attraction or destination, yet the quality of their tours can vary quite a bit. And the actual tour guides can be 100 percent different: One can know everything and the next one is on his or her first day on the job. Ultimately, the difference between bad and great tours is the result of one person.

## Non-Negotiable Travel Rules for Tour Guides

1. Check the guide's language skills before you pay. Just because they say the tour guide speaks English does not mean he or she does.

2. Buying a tour online normally costs 2-10 times more.

3. Good tour company guides have published YouTube videos about the tours.

4. Private, guided tours are 3-5 times more dangerous than group tours.

5. You do not need a tour guide to visit an open-air market. Remember this when they drop you off to go shopping.

6.  Guides need to sleep in same hotels as clients.

7.  Look at the transportation before you pay for the tour.

8.  Do not fall in love with the guide.

9.  Half the fun of a tour is meeting the people on the tour.

## Advisable Travel Rules for Tour Guides

10. It is better to read about a tour destination after the tour.

11. Do not allow friends of the tour guide to come along. They will spend their time talking, which diminishes the value of the tour.

**Go online to add more rules or corrections to this topic; we will credit you in future additions. TheRulesofTravel.com/28**

# About Andy Lee Graham

Andy Lee Graham grew up in Orland, Indiana, a Midwestern U.S. city of 400 people. HE spent his youth playing sports: football, basketball, and pole vaulting. After graduating from a high school of only 130 students, he went on to Indiana University, where he studied philosophy and psychology.

Those first years after university were tumultuous. Andy drank too much, never married, and never quite found his stride. But he was always an entrepreneur at heart and started many small businesses, from light furniture manufacturing to real estate sales and investments.

In 1997 at age 42, Andy traveled to Mexico for a six-week vacation. While lying on the beach in Pie de La Cuesta, Mexico (about 8 miles north of Acapulco), he met a Norwegian girl and fell in love with travel, or maybe the girl. The path is never clear.

Andy went home to Indiana, dumped all his worldly possessions, and flew to Belize to meet up again with her. Meanwhile, the travel addiction was finding a new addict. After a few months in Mexico, he started moving south, writing a weekly newsletter as he spent the next five years meandering through Central and South America. And after five years of travel, the addiction is almost irreversible; it is in his blood. He is a real traveler.

In 2000, while staying in the Voyager Hostel in Panama, Andy purchased the domain name, HoboTraveler.com, and became Andy the Hobo Traveler, writer and travel website owner.

When the Iraq war broke out, he started a daily blog teaching others how to travel into a dangerous country. The newsletter went from a weekly publication to a daily blog. Although his writing craftsmanship could be weak – being a bit dyslexic and prone to grammar errors – his readership grew quickly. He enjoyed traveling to places where other travelers refused to venture and writing about them, and readers loved his tales and tips.

After monetizing his website with Google Adsense, HoboTraveler.com grew as a business. Andy was no longer a poor backpacker, but, instead, making 2-3 times the average American income. He was able to buy plane tickets to anywhere and everywhere, and during his 16 plus years of nonstop travel, Andy has circled the planet at least 20 times.

Now, more than 16 years and 90 countries later, Andy has found his vocation, his calling in life: He is a perpetual world traveler.

Does Andy also consider himself a professional author? The answer is no. He says he is, first and foremost, a world traveler. He just happens to enjoy writing, photographing, and videographing about living his dream travel life and helping others to enjoy it, too.

Now age 58 (born in 1955), Andy Lee Graham is an old-timer of world travel, quite possibly the longest perpetual traveler living on the planet. And he has no plans to ever stop traveling.

CPSIA information can be obtained
at www.ICGtesting.com
Printed in the USA
LVOW13s1623150517
534584LV00007B/686/P